Introduction to Risk Management

Warren T. Hope

First Edition • Eighth Printing
American Institute for Chartered Property Casualty
Underwriters/Insurance Institute of America
720 Providence Road, Suite 100
Malvern, PA 19355-3433

Foreword

The American Institute for Chartered Property Casualty Underwriters and the Insurance Institute of America (the Institutes) are independent, not-for-profit organizations committed to expanding the knowledge of professionals in risk management, insurance, financial services, and related fields through education and research.

In accordance with our belief that professionalism is grounded ineducation experience, and ethical behavior, the Institutes provide a wide range of educational programs designed to meet the needs of individuals working in property-casualty insurance and risk management. The American Institute offers the Chartered Property Casualty Underwriter (CPCU®) professional designation. You select a specialization in the CPCU program with either a commercial or a personal risk management and insurance focus, depending on your professional needs. In addition to this specialization, the CPCU program gives you a broad understanding of the property-casualty insurance industry.

The Insurance Institute of America (IIA) offers designations and certificate programs in a wide range of disciplines, including the following:

- Claims
- Commercial underwriting
- Fidelity and surety bonding
- General insurance
- Insurance accounting and finance
- Insurance information technology
- Insurance production and agency management
- Insurance regulation and compliance
- Management
- Marine insurance
- Personal insurance
- Premium auditing
- Quality insurance services
- Reinsurance
- Risk managemen
- Surplus lines

No matter which Institute program you choose, you will gain practical knowledge and skills that will help you to grow personally and professionally.

The American Institute for CPCU was founded in 1942 through a collaborative effort between industry professionals and academics, led by the faculty members at The Wharton School of the University of Pennsylvania. In 1953, the American Institute for CPCU merged with the IIA, which was founded in 1909 and which remains the oldest continuously functioning national organization offering educational programs for the property-casualty insurance business. The Institutes continuously strive to maximize the value of your education and qualifications in the expanding insurance market. In 2005, the Institutes extended their global reach by forming the CPCU Institute of Greater China (CPCUIGC). In addition, many CPCU and IIA courses now qualify for credits towards certain associate's, bachelor's, and master's degrees at several prestigious colleges and universities, and all CPCU and IIA courses carry college credit recommendations from the American Council on Education (ACE).

The Insurance Research Council (IRC), founded in 1977, helps the Institutes fulfill the research aspect of their mission. The IRC is a division of the Institutes and is supported by industry members. The IRC is a not-for-profit research organization that examines public policy issues of interest to property-casualty insurers, insurance customers, and the general public. IRC research reports are distributed widely to insurance-related organizations, public policy authorities, and the media.

Our textbooks are an essential component of the education we provide. Each book is specifically designed both to provide you with the practical knowledge and skills you need to enhance your job performance and career and also to deliver that knowledge in a clear manner. The content is developed by the Institutes in collaboration with insurance and risk management professionals and members of the academic community. We welcome comments from our students and course leaders because your feedback helps us to continuously improve the quality of our study materials. Through our combined efforts, we will truly be *succeeding together*.

Peter L. Miller, CPCU
President and CEO
American Institute for CPCU
Insurance Institute of America

Introduction

Everything you need to study the American Institute for CPCU/Insurance Institute of America's Introduction to Risk Management course and prepare for the exam is in this book. It includes six assignments, a glossary, sample questions similar to those that are likely to appear on the exam, and answers to those questions.

Each of the six assignments is made up of three sections: introductory material; a chapter of assigned study material; and Review Questions and Exercises. You will gain most from this course if you use all three sections of each assignment.

The introductory material provides a preview of each assignment. Each brief statement headed "Before You Begin" explains the purpose of the assignment. The Educational Objectives indicate what you should gain from your study of each assignment. The outlines indicate how the assigned reading material is organized. Some students might find it beneficial to use the Educational Objectives or outlines as a basis for organizing their notes.

Although the reading assignments are relatively brief, they should be read and studied with some care, more than once. The Review Questions and Exercises are designed to help you achieve the Educational Objectives by urging you to look at the study material from a number of points of view and to experiment with working with that material. In some cases, the questions and exercises will send you back to the study material (or to the glossary) to get specific information, reconsider some passages, or check your answers.

The result of the use of these three sections of each assignment should be a rapid but concentrated introduction to the risk management process and to the techniques used in applying that process, giving you a sense of what risk managers do, how they go about doing it, and why what they do is important. It should also provide you with a basic understanding of how risk management fits in organizational structures and how it helps a wide range of organizations to achieve their goals. But it must be emphasized that *this course is only an introduction*. No one will learn to be a risk manager merely by studying this course.

Students can study this course and prepare for the exam independently, by forming or joining a study group, or by attending class. For some students, joining a study group or attending class will be a valuable supplement to the Review Questions and Exercises, providing them with the chance to compare notes, opinions, and answers with others who are interested in risk management. Nonetheless, all three methods of study and exam preparation can be effective. Students should decide for themselves the method that suits them best.

The idea for the course originated with members of the Advisory Committee of the Institutes' Associate in Risk Management (ARM) designation program and Dr. George L. Head, CPCU, CLU, ARM. I am particularly grateful to Dr. Head and two of his committee members, Frederick B. Molineux, JD, CPCU, ARM and Steven B. Steinberg, CPCU, ARM, for their interest in and support of this course. They freely shared ideas, offered suggestions, and kindly agreed to review and comment on the manuscript for this book. Although they cannot be held responsible for the book's final form in any way, they certainly helped to make it better than it otherwise might have been.

I cannot take sole responsibility for what this book says and how it says it. It would have been a completely different book without the work of the contributing authors, who are listed on a separate page. Although their work primarily appears in Chapters 1, 5, and 6, it necessarily shaped and influenced the whole book. They also reviewed various drafts of the entire manuscript.

For more information about the Institutes' programs, please call our Customer Support Department at (800) 644-2101, e-mail us at customersupport@cpcuiia.org, or visit our Web site at www.aicpcu.org.

Warren T. Hope

Contributing Authors

The American Institute for CPCU and the Insurance Institute of America acknowledge, with deep appreciation, the contributions of the following authors:

Jane Combrinck-Graham, JD, CPCU
Director of Resources
Aon Risk Services, Inc. of Pennsylvania

Karen L. Hamilton, PhD, CPCU, CLU
Director of Curriculum
American Institute for Chartered Property Casualty Underwriters
Insurance Institute of America

John Kelly, CPCU, ARM, AAI
Sections Manager
CPCU Society

Contents

Assignment *1*

BEFORE YOU BEGIN

Since you are reading this book, you probably have some interest in risk management. Perhaps you know or work with someone who has the title "Risk Manager," or maybe you noticed the section entitled "Risk Manager of the Year" as you flipped through a copy of *Business Insurance*. You may have marveled at the seeming complexity of the tasks performed by risk managers and may even have wondered exactly what risk managers do and how they do it.

This course introduces you to the field of risk management—what risk managers do, how they do it, and why risk management is important.

This assignment begins with some basics. Understanding some fundamental terms and concepts will do much to help you have a clearer idea of what risk management is and why it is important. These basics will also help prepare you for the later assignments in this course.

EDUCATIONAL OBJECTIVES FOR ASSIGNMENT 1

After completing this assignment, you should be able to:

1. Define or explain a number of fundamental risk management terms and concepts.

2. Describe how loss exposures are classified for risk management purposes.

3. Explain why risk management is important for individuals, organizations, and society.

OUTLINE OF REQUIRED READING

Chapter 1
The Basics

Risk management has become a popular term that is not always used in the same way. You might have heard the term on the evening news, when the anchorperson announced that a local government had gotten into financial trouble through "poor risk management," meaning that the government had made some unwise investments. You might also have heard the term in a popular movie in which "risk management" was blamed for a car maker's decision to defend lawsuits rather than recall and repair defective cars. To understand just what risk management is and why it is important, it will help to begin with a definition.

WHAT IS RISK MANAGEMENT?

The easy answer to that question is that risk management is the way individuals and organizations manage risk. The trouble with that definition, of course, is that it uses the terms we want to define in the definition.

Management is a common term that most people understand. At its root it means "handling." It seems to have been originally applied by the Romans to training horses. Now it refers to all kinds of things—handling problems or personnel, handling manufacturing processes, or handling personal finances. The word still carries the sense of curbing or controlling what would otherwise be out of control.

Risk is a less common term. In risk management, it is used in a specific way. **Risk** means uncertainty about whether a loss will occur. It consists of two key elements—uncertainty and loss. This definition can be clarified with an example.

> **Risk** means uncertainty about whether a loss will occur.

Risk: An Example

Suppose you were to climb into your car and drive to your favorite restaurant. Although you might not think about it very much, you would be encountering risk. While driving, you *could* become involved in an accident—and that accident could result in loss.

The loss could involve any or all of the following:

- Damage to your auto, which would lessen its value and require money to be spent to repair the damage or replace the auto

- Bodily injury to you, which might keep you from doing your job and earning wages

- Damage to the other party's auto or bodily injury to the other party, for which you might be required to compensate that person

Statistically speaking, you probably would arrive at your favorite restaurant without being involved in an auto accident. But the possibility of an accident exists, and it is *uncertain whether an auto accident and the losses that result will occur.* If you decide to drive to your favorite restaurant, the *risk* of an auto accident exists.

If it were statistically impossible for a loss to occur, no uncertainty about the occurrence of loss would exist. In that case, there would be no risk. Suppose a business decided to stop manufacturing widgets and never again entered the widget-manufacturing business. The probability of the business suffering a loss of profit because the selling price of widgets fell to a price below the cost of manufacturing a widget is zero. Since the business no longer manufactures widgets, it does not face the *risk* of loss of profit from widget sales at those low prices.

Some people and businesses thrive on risk. Businesspeople often recognize that they must take chances to be successful. On the other hand, some people and businesses have little appetite for risk. Some are so averse to risk that they will avoid situations involving the possibility of loss, even if the potential gains could be very rewarding. You no doubt will continue to drive to your favorite restaurant—the relatively slight risk is offset by the clear gain. The business that chose to stop manufacturing widgets might regret its decision when competitors are highly successful because of a widget price increase.

Risk Management Defined

Most people and businesses are willing to accept a certain amount of risk if they feel they can manage or handle it. **Risk management** is the process to best handle uncertainty about whether losses will occur. Risk can be made acceptable by managing it. Being able to manage, in this case, means *trying to prevent losses, trying to decrease the frequency or severity of losses, or paying for those losses that occur despite our best*

> **Risk management** is the process to best handle uncertainty about whether losses will occur.

efforts. **Loss frequency** refers to how often losses occur and is used to predict how likely they are to occur. **Loss severity** refers to the amount of damage resulting from losses and how much it will cost to pay for losses. The severity of losses is used to predict how costly future losses are likely to be.

> **Loss frequency** refers to how often losses occur and is used to predict the likelihood of similar losses in the future.

Types of Risk

In general, there are two types of risks—pure risks and speculative risks. These two types of risk are based on the possible outcomes that can result from uncertainty about whether losses will occur.

> **Loss severity** refers to the amount of damage resulting from losses and is used to predict how costly future losses are likely to be.

A **pure risk** can only result in a loss or no loss. A pure risk presents no opportunity for gain. If no loss occurs when you drive to your favorite restaurant, you are in the same financial position as you were when you set out— your car is undamaged, you are uninjured, and no other car or person has been damaged or injured. The risk of an auto accident is a pure risk.

> A **pure risk** can only result in a loss or no loss. A pure risk presents no opportunity for gain.

A **speculative risk**, on the other hand, can result in loss, no loss, or gain. That widget manufacturer might own stock in other corporations. The value of that stock could decline, causing a loss, or increase, producing a gain. The risk of a possible change in stock prices is a speculative risk.

> A **speculative risk** can result in loss, no loss, or gain.

Another way of distinguishing between these two types of risk is to say that *pure risks* represent uncertainties about whether *accidental* losses will occur. *Speculative risks* arise from activities that are *intentionally* engaged in because they might result in a gain.

Traditionally, risk management was concerned only with pure risks. Risk management was developed as a way to handle the uncertainty of whether accidental losses would occur. Now risk management is sometimes seen as a broader function, one that can also help in handling speculative risks. After all, from the point of view of a business, a loss is a loss, no matter how it comes about. This course focuses on how pure risks are handled. But you should realize that the techniques described in this text can also be adapted to help handle speculative risks.

LOSSES, LOSS EXPOSURES, AND RISK MANAGEMENT

All of us at some time in our lives have lost something of value—CDs left in the trunk of a car that were warped beyond playability by the hot summer sun, or a bike that was stolen from the front porch. The loss that was heartbreaking at the time may have been forgotten as the years passed.

You might have marveled at how risk managers accomplish their complex jobs.

Courtesy of Sentry Insurance.

Other losses are of a much more serious nature and could change or even end a person's or a business's life. People can be killed in auto accidents. Businesses can be bankrupted by economic downturns.

> A **loss** occurs when an item of property or a right owned by a person or an organization has declined in value, or a capacity to perform has been diminished.

A **loss** occurs when an item of property or a right owned by a person or an organization has declined in value, or when a capacity to perform has been diminished. If fire destroys a pizzeria, the owner will suffer a property loss—the pizzeria itself. If zoning laws have changed since the pizzeria opened for business, the owner could lose the right to reopen at that location. If a baker were injured during the fire, the pizzeria's capacity to reopen could diminish, and the baker's capacity to earn wages might be lost or limited. All of these possible consequences of the fire are losses. Risk management tries to prevent those losses, tries to decrease the frequency or severity of such losses, or pays for those losses that do occur. The emphasis on *value* in the definition of loss helps to target the kinds of losses with which risk management is primarily concerned—accidental losses that have measurable financial consequences.

> **Loss exposures** are possibilities of accidental losses with measurable financial consequences.

Loss exposures are possibilities of accidental losses with measurable financial consequences. This idea is fundamental to what risk managers and others involved in risk management do. They try to prevent losses, try to decrease their frequency or severity, or finance them by identifying loss exposures and analyzing them. Every individual or organization faces a wide variety of loss exposures. One way to start handling this wide variety of exposures is by classifying them into types.

Types of Loss Exposures

A loss exposure consists of three elements—a *value* that can be diminished or destroyed by a specific *cause* with *financial consequences for a specific entity*, a person or an organization. This idea will become clearer if we reconsider the losses that the pizzeria fire mentioned above might have caused (see Exhibit 1-1).

Exhibit 1-1
Four Types of Loss Exposures

• Property	• Personnel
• Liability	• Net income

The cause of loss, sometimes called the **peril**, is the same in each case—fire. Nonetheless, the four types of loss exposures—property loss exposures, liability loss exposures, personnel loss exposures, and net income loss exposures—were all potentially present because of the various values involved.

> A **peril** is a cause of loss.

Property Loss Exposures

The building that houses the pizzeria and everything in it has value. Ownership of that building and the things it contains—sometimes called its *contents*—represents a **property** loss exposure, a possibility of accidental loss with measurable financial consequences for the owner. If the fire damaged or destroyed that building or its contents, the owner of that property would suffer an economic loss. The owner would either have to do without the use of the destroyed or damaged property or pay to repair or replace it.

> **Real property** means land, buildings, and other structures attached to the land. **Personal property** includes everything but real property. Furniture, fixtures, and inventory are examples of personal property. Ownership of real or personal property constitutes a **property loss exposure**.

Liability Loss Exposures

Liability means that an individual or organization is legally responsible—liable—for the injury or damage suffered by another person or organization. The fire at the pizzeria could cause injuries to other people, neighbors or passersby, for instance. The owner of the pizzeria could be held liable for those injuries to others. Operating the pizzeria represents a liability loss exposure, the possibility of an accidental loss to another individual or organization with measurable financial

> **Liability** means that an individual or organization is legally responsible—liable—for the injury or damage suffered by another person or organization.

consequences. The risk to the operator of the pizzeria of being liable for the injuries suffered by other people as a result of the fire constitutes a liability loss exposure. Even the possibility of being sued represents a liability loss exposure, regardless of whether you win the suit, because defending a lawsuit is expensive.

Personnel Loss Exposures

Personnel are crucial to the success of most businesses. Employing personnel represents a personnel loss exposure, a situation that can lead to a loss with measurable financial consequences. If a baker was injured in the fire at the pizzeria, diminishing the business's capacity to reopen, the employer of the baker would suffer the economic loss involved in replacing or augmenting the baker's services.

> Employing personnel represents a **personnel loss exposure** through the possible death, disability, or injury of an employee.

Net Income Loss Exposures

Net income is defined as the amount of revenues over expenses that is generated in a specific accounting period—a calendar year, for instance. A change in the zoning laws since the time when the pizzeria first opened could prevent the owner from reopening at the same location after the fire. Such a change in the zoning laws could result in a net income loss—revenues could be drastically reduced and expenses increased while the owner tried to reestablish the business at a new location. The right to operate the pizzeria at its current location represents a net income loss exposure, a situation that could lead to an accidental loss

> **Net income** is defined as the amount of revenues over expenses that is generated in a specific accounting period.

with measurable financial consequences. If that right were lost, the owner of that right would suffer an economic loss; he would either have to go out of business or suffer the decreased revenues and increased expenses of starting over again elsewhere.

Exhibit 1-2
Elements of a Loss Exposure

- Value exposed to loss—property, liability, personnel, net income
- Cause of loss or peril
- Financial consequences

Uses of the Types of Loss Exposures

Classifying loss exposures into these four types—property loss exposures, liability loss exposures, personnel loss exposures, and net income loss exposures—helps people involved in risk management to prevent losses, decrease their frequency or severity, or finance them by understanding both the values and the causes of loss involved. (See Exhibit 1-2 to review the elements of a loss exposure.) Later chapters of this text will cover the uses of the types of loss exposures and the relationship between values and causes of loss. For now, you should know and be able to explain the four types of loss exposures.

WHY RISK MANAGEMENT IS IMPORTANT

As you no doubt realize after this quick look at the basics of risk management, handling uncertainties about whether losses will occur can be a complex and involved undertaking. This is especially true for large organizations that face a bewildering number and variety of loss exposures. Is it worth the effort? Why is risk management important?

First, risk management prevents or reduces losses. Risk management's ability to anticipate and limit the financial consequences of losses is a primary benefit for individuals, organizations, and society at large. In addition, risk management finds predictable ways to pay for those losses that do occur.

Risk Management Benefits:

- Prevention of losses
- Reduction of the financial consequences of losses
- Peace of mind

Individuals and organizations are relieved of at least some of the emotional and financial burden of losses. The ability to handle the possibilities of loss enables individuals and organizations to survive and thrive when they might otherwise face unendurable burdens. Reducing uncertainty to a manageable level is essential for the survival of any business enterprise and many other organizations.

Society also benefits from the prevention or reduction of losses because fewer and less costly losses mean that more funds are available for other uses, uses that can spur economic growth.

Beyond that, managing risk increases peace of mind. Thanks to risk management, individuals and organizations actively control potential losses. This element of control reduces the amount of anxiety experienced because of the possibility of loss and enables individuals and organizations to engage in worthwhile activities they might otherwise avoid.

SUMMARY

The purpose of this chapter was simply to introduce you to the basics, some fundamental risk management terms and concepts—risk, loss, loss exposures, and so on. You will find these terms and ideas turning up time and again throughout this text. They make up the language of risk management, and learning that language now will help you as you proceed through this course.

Risk management means handling uncertainty about whether a loss will occur. The primary way risk management does this is by treating loss exposures, possibilities of loss. In order to start thinking about how best to treat loss exposures, it is helpful to classify them based on the types of values exposed to loss—property, liability, personnel, and net income. All loss exposures faced by individuals and organizations can be grouped into one or more of these four types of loss exposures. Loss exposures are further analyzed based on causes of loss (or perils) and the financial consequences of a loss for a specific individual or organization. Values, causes of loss, and the financial consequences of loss constitute the three elements of a loss exposure.

Several benefits flow from the practice of risk management, not only for the individual or organization that practices risk management but also for others and society at large. The three primary benefits of risk management are prevention of losses; reduction of the financial consequences of losses; and peace of mind, a reduction of the anxiety caused by potential losses.

The remaining chapters in this text will introduce you to the risk management process and enable you to see it at work in a number of settings. One of the things that you should take away from this course is the sense that risk management is an activity accomplished by various people working together for a specific purpose, to handle the uncertainty about whether losses will occur.

REVIEW QUESTIONS AND EXERCISES

1. Define or describe each of the words and phrases listed below:

    (a) Risk

    (b) Risk management

    (c) Pure risk

    (d) Speculative risk

    (e) Loss

    (f) Loss frequency

    (g) Loss severity

    (h) Loss exposure

    (i) Peril

    (j) Real property

    (k) Personal property

    (l) Liability

    (m) Net income

    (n) Personnel loss exposure

    (o) Benefits of risk management

    After writing your definitions or explanations, compare them with the definitions in the Glossary at the back of this book.

2.   Name and briefly describe the four types of loss exposures.

3.   Classify each of the following as either (a) a pure risk, (b) a speculative risk, or (c) unclassi-
fiable based on the information given:

(a) the possibility that a house you own will be damaged or destroyed by earthquake

(b) the possibility that the market value of a house you own will be other than the price you
paid for it

(c) the possibility that a business you own will be found legally liable for injury to a customer
from a product that your business manufactures

(d) the possibility that a business you own might gain or lose an important contract to supply
services

4. Classify each of the following loss exposures as (a) property, (b) liability, (c) personnel, or (d) net income:

(a) Jim might damage his car if it skids on an icy road and hits a tree.

(b) Jim might cause injury to a passenger in his car as a result of the accident described in (a) above.

(c) Jim might be injured in the accident and be unable to work.

(d) Sarah owns an apartment house that might be damaged by a hurricane.

(e) Sarah might lose rental income from her tenants because of damage caused by the hurricane.

ANSWERS TO ASSIGNMENT 1 QUESTIONS

1. (Define key terms.)

2. The four types of loss exposures:

   - Property loss exposure—The possibility of loss to real property (land, buildings, and other structures attached to the land) and personal property (all property other than real property)

   - Liability loss exposure—The possibility of a loss that an individual or organization incurs when legally responsible for the injury or damage suffered by another person or organization

   - Personnel loss exposure—The possibility of a loss because of the death, disability, or injury of an employee

   - Net income loss exposure—The possibility of a loss of net income (the amount revenues that exceed expenses)

3. Classifications of the following risks:

   - Possibility of earthquake damage to or destruction of a house—pure risk

   - Possibility that the market value of a house you own will be other than the price you paid for it—speculative risk

   - Possibility of a business's legal liability for injury to a customer from a product manufactured by the business—pure risk

   - Possibility that a business may gain or lose an important contract to supply services—speculative risk

4. Classifications of the following loss exposures:

   - Damage to Jim's car if it skids on an icy road and hits a tree—property loss exposure

   - Injury to a passenger in Jim's car as a result of the accident—liability loss exposure

   - Jim's injuries in the accident and his subsequent inability to work—personnel loss exposure

   - Hurricane damage to Sarah's apartment house—property loss exposure

   - Loss of rental income from Sarah's tenants because of hurricane damage to her apartment house—net income loss exposure

Assignment 2

BEFORE YOU BEGIN

In the first assignment, risk management was defined as a way of handling uncertainty about whether a loss will occur. This assignment will look at risk management as a process, a specific and systematic sequence of steps. You will see that process in action as it is applied to a common activity as you read a discussion of it. Assignment 1 gave you a general idea of what risk management is. This assignment will introduce you to how risk managers and others go about managing risks. The Review Questions and Exercises at the end of the assignment will help you focus on what is most important for you to learn and help you achieve the Educational Objectives.

EDUCATIONAL OBJECTIVES FOR ASSIGNMENT 2

After completing this assignment, you should be able to:

1. Identify and describe the steps in the risk management process.

2. Identify and describe the tools and methods used for exposure identification and analysis.

3. Identify and describe the primary techniques available for treating loss exposures.

4. Explain how you might use the risk management process to handle the loss exposures you face by owning and operating a car.

OUTLINE OF REQUIRED READING

I. The Drive to Work

II. The Risk Management Process
  A. Identifying and analyzing loss exposures
    1. Property loss exposures
    2. Values
    3. Causes of loss
  B. Financial consequences for Rita
    1. Rita's other loss exposures
    2. Liability loss exposures
    3. Hazards
      a. Preparations at home
      b. Preparations in the parking lot
      c. Local driving
      d. Interstate driving
      e. City driving
      f. Parking at work
  C. Examining the feasibility of alternative techniques
    1. Risk control techniques
    2. Risk financing techniques
  D. Selecting the most appropriate techniques
    1. Rita's mini-risk management program
    2. Coordination of recommendations
  E. Implementing the chosen techniques
  F. Monitoring and improving the risk management program

III. Summary

Chapter **2**

Risk Management on the Road

You already practice risk management. Everybody does. We all face the possibility of loss and must handle the uncertainty that it causes. Most of us handle risk through a combination of instinct, habit, and common sense. We are often unaware that we are handling uncertainty even when we are doing so. Risk managers and others who perform the risk management function—small business owners, the chief financial officers of corporations, people in professions or occupations with an exceptionally high degree of risk, and insurance agents, brokers, and consultants—differ from the rest of us in two fundamental ways: first, they are very much aware of the need to manage risks; second, they use a systematic method of handling risks—the risk management process.

This chapter will introduce you to the risk management process by examining an activity most of us perform on a regular basis, driving to work.

THE DRIVE TO WORK

Rita McGoff has been working at Urban University for almost eight years, ever since she graduated from high school. During that time, Rita, having taken classes at night, earned a Bachelor of Science degree in Business with a concentration in management from Urban. Urban's free tuition policy for employees was one of the perks that attracted Rita to employment at the university, and that policy encouraged her to continue working there.

Rita has also received a number of promotions and job changes as a member of the university's staff. Her first job was in the accounts receivable section of the university's Financial Services Department. She is now a Legal Affairs Coordinator, working with the attorneys of the university's legal staff. She sometimes thinks that she might like to go to law school.

Rita celebrated her most recent promotion by buying a new car for about $17,000. After driving a series of aged but serviceable cars, she is very proud of her car, even if the bank owns more of it than she does.

If society were organized to suit Rita, the business day would not start before 10 A.M. and she would never go to sleep before midnight. Rita is not a morning person, but she has adjusted reasonably well, making do with orange juice, toast, and coffee at the counter of the kitchen in her apartment with the radio playing before going to work. The music helps her get ready for the day, and she listens to the weather and the traffic report while she eats as a way of preparing for the commute to Urban's campus, twenty miles away.

In the parking lot of Rita's apartment complex, she glances at the tires of her car before opening the door. Several years ago she had found that she had a flat tire. That had been enough to throw off the whole morning, so she now routinely checks the tires each morning.

Seated behind the wheel of the car, she slides her second cup of coffee of the day into the beverage rack below the radio, puts on her seat belt, and starts the engine. She checks the fuel and other gauges on the dash while turning the radio on and then taking a sip of coffee.

She spends seven minutes in stop-and-go traffic in the suburb where she lives. The speed limit there is twenty-five miles per hour and she is aware of her tendency to drift up to thirty-five or forty mph. A local policeman once noticed this tendency too and drew it to her attention by giving her a ticket that required her to pay a surprisingly high fine. One intersection she passes through every day on her way to the interstate irritates Rita. She once was able to sail through it because the traffic on the cross street had stop signs. There was a number of accidents at the intersection, maybe because the stopped drivers became impatient and took unnecessary chances. The intersection now has four-way stop signs, and it irritates Rita that no one now seems to know who has the right of way. Cars at all four corners seem to sit there while the drivers look at each other and then simultaneously inch into the intersection and then stop again. Rita wrote to the local traffic authority requesting that a light be put up at the intersection, but nothing has come of that.

About seven minutes after leaving home, Rita turns right onto the interstate. She drives at the speed limit—65 mph in some places, 55 in others—on the interstate for about twenty minutes to reach the exit that is closest to Urban's campus. After four minutes of driving in heavy city traffic after leaving the interstate, Rita arrives at her parking spot in a lot reserved for employees at Urban's campus. The Legal Affairs office is a short walk from her parking spot.

If all goes well, the commute takes Rita just over half an hour. She starts work at 8:30 A.M. and invariably leaves her apartment by 7:45. When she locks the door to her car and throws the empty cardboard coffee cup into the trash receptacle in the parking lot, she feels ready to start the day and walks quickly to her office.

THE RISK MANAGEMENT PROCESS

Risk managers apply the risk management process when they do their jobs. The risk management process is based on the scientific method and is similar to the process used for making general business decisions. The risk management process consists of a sequence of five logical, systematic steps:

1. Identifying and analyzing loss exposures

2. Examining the feasibility of alternative techniques available for treating those exposures

3. Selecting the most appropriate combination of those techniques

4. Implementing the selected techniques

5. Monitoring results and considering the need for change or improvement

Let's look at how the risk management process might be applied to Rita's commute.

Identifying and Analyzing Loss Exposures

The types of loss exposures described in Chapter 1—property loss exposures, liability loss exposures, personnel loss exposures, and net income loss exposures—provide a framework that aids in the identification and analysis of exposures.

You will recall that every loss exposure consists of three elements—a value; a potential cause of loss or peril; and the financial consequences of a loss for a specific *entity*, that is, *a person or an organization*. Identifying and analyzing the loss exposures Rita faces during her drive to work require discovering all of the values that might be decreased by various causes that would have financial consequences *for Rita*. Looking at her property loss exposures will clarify this point.

Property Loss Exposures

When managing Rita's risks, we are interested only in loss exposures to Rita's property. Of the two primary kinds of property, real and personal, Rita's commute exposes only her personal property, her new car and everything it contains, to loss. (She does not own real property—land, buildings, or other structures attached to land.)

Values

How could we go about determining precisely what Rita's personal property consists of?

The car is easy. But what about the contents?

We could ask Rita what's in the car or ask her to provide us with an inventory of the contents. We might also inspect the car ourselves, with Rita's permission, and make our own inventory of its contents—seven audiocassettes, an umbrella, two yellowed paperback mysteries, candy wrappers, a road map of the state of Maine, a snow shovel, and a sweatshirt along with roadside flares, a spare tire, and a jack in the trunk, and so on.

Asking Rita and inspecting her car for ourselves represent two widely used tools for identifying loss exposures: (1) *surveys* or *questionnaires* and (2) *inspections*. Professionals responsible for managing the risks of large corporations need sophisticated surveys and must inspect properties or processes that are much more complex than the contents of Rita's car. But no matter how simple or complex the exposures involved are, these tools work. They help to provide complete, credible, and objective information on which to base risk management decisions.

Causes of Loss

Think briefly about your own experiences as a car owner and driver.

What are the various ways your own car or its contents could be damaged, destroyed, or otherwise lost?

A short list no doubt comes to mind immediately. Another vehicle might hit you, you might run into another car or some other object (a telephone pole, for instance), the car could be stolen, and so on. Simply thinking about all of the possible causes of loss is another tool risk managers use to identify loss exposures—it is sometimes called brainstorming. But cars and their contents are so widespread that brainstorming is probably not the most efficient way of identifying their perils. A more efficient way is to (1) *review the losses that have occurred to others* or (2) *seek the advice of experts*. Rita probably used both of these exposure identification tools when she purchased auto insurance. Insurance companies, agents, and brokers have access to masses of sorted and analyzed data that relate to the losses arising from the ownership and use of an auto. The data have been translated into lists of perils or causes of loss that are probably more extensive and complete than any we could come up with through brainstorming.

Risk managers know they can't know everything. They are always willing to use the loss experience and expertise of others to supplement their own experience and knowledge. Like surveys and inspections, loss histories and the records or expertise of others can help assure that risk management decisions are based on objective, credible data.

Financial Consequences for Rita

The damage, destruction, or loss of Rita's car or its contents would have measurable financial consequences for her. In general terms, she would be faced with the alternative of either doing without the lost property (replacing the drive to work with a commute using public transportation) or paying to repair or replace that property (buying a new car or having her car repaired). Exposure identification and analysis require a dollar amount.

Risk managers frequently use tools to collect credible data on the costs of repairing or replacing property. The loss experience and expertise of others can help assess the financial consequences of the exposures as they can help with the identification of perils. In other words, Rita probably handled this element of her exposure too when she purchased personal auto insurance. But other methods could be used that we should consider briefly.

Rita borrowed money from a bank to buy her new car. Records of the loan would give us the price of the car at the time of the purchase. Because Rita's car is new, we could also learn how much money she would need to replace it by looking at the records of her purchase of the car or by asking dealers who sell cars of the same make, model, and year.

Body shops, auto repair shops, and insurance claims adjusters use manuals that would permit us to calculate how much it should cost to repair or replace almost any part or combination of parts of Rita's car.

Similarly, to calculate the financial consequences for Rita of loss of the contents of the car, we could rely on receipts that Rita might have from the purchase of the items in the car. If Rita does not have receipts, catalogs or visits to stores would enable us to establish prices for most if not all of the things on the inventory we prepared of the car's contents.

In short, risk managers rely on accounting and other records and documents, as well as the experience or expertise of others, to calculate the costs of repairing or replacing property. You can readily imagine that if Rita needed to replace her new car, the financial consequences of the property loss exposure she faces as a result of her drive to work could amount to $18,000 or more.

Rita's Other Loss Exposures

A risk manager would take this same systematic approach and use the same or similar tools to identify and analyze Rita's liability, personnel, and net income loss exposures arising from her commute. It will be most helpful to concentrate on the liability loss exposures Rita faces as a result of her drive to work. Net income and personnel exposures are most relevant for the risk management of organizations, rather than individuals, and will be considered in later chapters. We *could*, of course, look at Rita as an economic unit, an organization of one. She generates revenues (salary), she has expenses (bills), and the health and welfare of Rita McGoff are certainly crucial to Rita's success.

Liability Loss Exposures

Chapter 1 said that liability means that a person or organization is held legally responsible for the injury or damage suffered by another person or organization. The key word in this definition is "legally." Liability loss exposures are more difficult to identify and analyze than property loss exposures because of the types of losses potentially involved and the difficulty in measuring the financial consequences of those potential losses.

Consider the types of values involved: all of the people and property Rita could injure or damage during her drive to work, such as a child walking across the street, a store's plate glass window, or a school bus. Brainstorming is of little use in this situation if we wish to develop an exhaustive list of values.

Collision (Rita's car running into another person, vehicle, or object) is no doubt the primary cause of loss for the liability loss exposures Rita faces during her drive to work, but there are others. If Rita suffered a car fire, she might be held liable for damage caused to the property of others by the smoke from the fire, for instance.

The financial consequences for Rita are the most difficult element of her liability exposures to measure or predict. Financial consequences of liability losses can best be assessed with judgment, rather than measurement, possibly determined by a jury rather than, for instance, a catalog of used auto parts. It is perhaps sufficient to say that if Rita were found legally responsible for a multiple-vehicle accident on the interstate that resulted in the death or serious injury of another person, the financial (and emotional) consequences for Rita could be catastrophic. All the money Rita has and all the property she owns would not be enough to cover the expenses of such a loss.

The best method for analyzing Rita's liability exposures is to rely on the loss histories of people in similar circumstances and the expertise of others. Once again, Rita probably used this method when she purchased auto insurance. Insurance companies, agents, and brokers have access to large amounts of loss data that have been evaluated and analyzed. In fact, the data help to determine insurance policy language, conditions, and premiums. In other words, much of what a risk manager could do for Rita has been done by providers of insurance.

Hazards

A **hazard** is anything that increases the possible frequency or severity of a loss. For example, if a fire is a cause of loss, or peril, storing oily rags in a garage is a hazard—a practice that can increase the possible frequency or severity of a fire loss to that garage. As a result, hazards must be considered when analyzing exposures. Hazards can be clues to effective ways of treating loss exposures, the second step in the risk management process.

> A **hazard** is anything that increases the possible frequency or severity of a loss.

One common exposure identification tool or method we have not yet used, the preparation of a flowchart, might help us pinpoint the hazards Rita encounters on her drive to work.

Her drive can be divided into six segments:

• Preparations before leaving home

• Preparations before leaving her apartment complex's parking lot

• Local driving

• Interstate driving

• City driving

• Parking at work

Making a flowchart entails displaying these segments graphically. A sketch like the one in Exhibit 2-1 will serve the purpose.

Exhibit 2-1
Flowchart

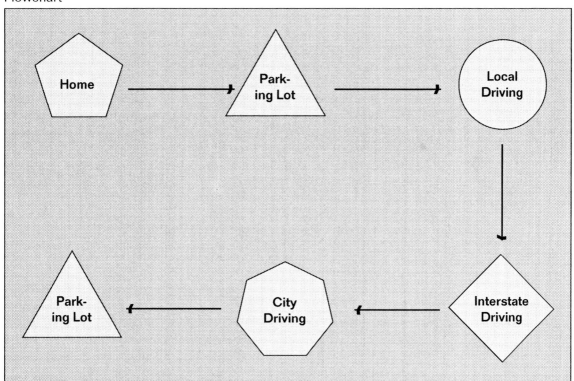

For each of these segments, we should consider and list each activity that could influence the likely frequency or severity of a loss.

Preparations at Home   Remember that Rita is not a morning person. She needs to be fully awake and alert before she begins her drive. Also remember that she listens to the weather and traffic reports on the radio each morning. Doing so could decrease the likelihood of an accident by allowing her to plan to take an alternate route to work if she learns that her usual route is closed or congested or by allowing her to take extra precautions and allow extra time because of weather conditions that present hazards—ice, snow, fog, and so on. But Rita allows herself only forty-five minutes to make a trip that takes more than half an hour if all goes well. Taking an alternate route or reducing speed to accommodate icy roads is likely to mean that Rita will be late for work. Too little time for the trip can be a hazard.

Preparations in the Parking Lot   Rita routinely glances at the tires of her car because she once came out in the morning and found a flat. She also checks the fuel and other gauges on the dashboard. This routine, cursory inspection shows that Rita realizes that both the car and the driver must be in good operating condition. This inspection could reduce the likely frequency or severity of accidents. Once again, though, the discovery of a mechanical problem would throw off Rita's entire schedule—another good reason for her to start out earlier on her drive to work.

Also Rita has her second cup of coffee while driving. Although this has become a widespread practice, it constitutes a hazard; she is unlikely to be able to react to an unusual circumstance as rapidly or as well as she otherwise might if she has a hot cup of coffee in one hand. (As recent, highly publicized court cases have shown, hot cups of coffee can be perils, causes of loss, as well as hazards. Rita could accidentally burn herself by spilling the coffee.) On the other hand, Rita does use her seat belt. This practice could reduce the severity of a loss resulting from an accident in which Rita's car is involved.

Local Driving   Rita is aware of her tendency to speed in her own neighborhood, a hazard likely to increase both the frequency and severity of an auto accident. She has already received a ticket for speeding and had to pay a fine. The payment of that fine can be seen as a net income loss for Rita, an additional expense associated with her drive to work.

Rita is also aware of her irritation at one specific intersection. It used to be a throughway with stop signs only on the cross street. But it is now equipped with four-way stop signs, and drivers seem reluctant to be the first to enter the intersection. She took the sensible step of urging that a traffic light be erected at the intersection. But until such an action is taken, Rita's irritation and the confusion of the other drivers at this intersection constitute a hazard, a condition that could increase the potential frequency of accidents at that intersection. (Of course, the four-way stop signs could represent an improvement, a step that will possibly decrease the severity of accidents at that intersection.)

Interstate Driving   Interstate driving is routinely the most hazard-free segment of Rita's drive. She stays within the speed limit and frequently finishes her coffee before she reaches the interstate. Traffic problems, weather conditions, road repairs, and accidents involving other vehicles are the most likely hazards she will encounter during this part of her trip.

City Driving   We have not been told that Rita speeds when she drives through the city, and the density of the traffic she encounters in the city might decrease the likelihood of her doing so. But she has displayed a tendency to exceed the speed limit when she is not on the interstate, and the shift from the interstate to city streets might heighten that tendency. If so, speeding would again be a hazard for this segment of her journey.

Parking at Work   Rita is fortunate in that she has an on-campus parking lot in which to leave her car while she is at work. The car is less likely to be damaged or stolen there than it would be if it had to be parked on the street far from Rita and her coworkers. Rita also routinely locks her car, a simple way to decrease the likelihood of theft.

Listing these hazards on the flowchart will prepare us for the second step in the risk management process—considering the various techniques available for treating the exposures.

Exhibit 2-2
Flowchart With Hazards in Place

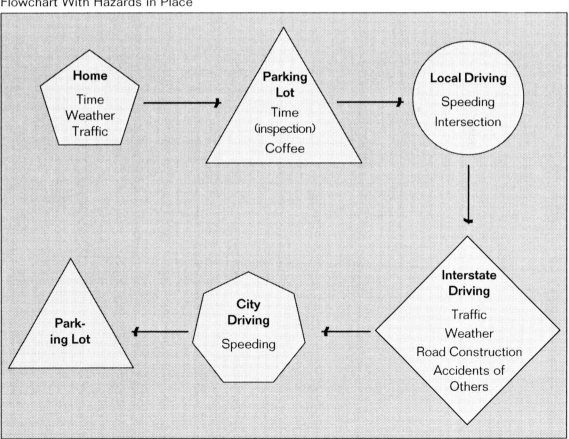

Examining the Feasibility of Alternative Techniques

There are two categories of risk management techniques for treating loss exposures: risk control techniques and risk financing techniques. *Risk control* techniques are intended to prevent losses, to minimize the frequency or severity of losses, or to make losses more predictable. *Risk financing* techniques are intended to pay for those losses that occur despite the best risk control efforts.

Risk Control Techniques

Basically, there are five risk control techniques:

1. Avoidance

2. Loss prevention

3. Loss reduction

4. Segregation of exposures

5. Contractual transfer of an asset or activity

Let's get a clearer idea of what these techniques include and how they can be used by evaluating their usefulness for Rita during her drive to work.

Avoidance involves choosing not to own an asset or engage in an activity that gives rise to the possibility of loss.

Avoidance is the most complete and often the least practical of risk management techniques. Someone can eliminate the possibility of loss by choosing not to own an asset or not to engage in an activity that gives rise to the possibility of loss, also known as the loss exposure. Avoidance would require Rita to give up entirely the use of her car for getting to work, not something that she would be likely to do even if she had another way of getting to work, such as public transportation.

Avoidance is a much more practical technique for large organizations with several alternatives available to them. A manufacturer of a large and complete line of tools that decides to introduce a new product—a specific kind of hand-held power saw, for instance—might choose to abandon the manufacture of that new product if it causes injuries to consumers, giving rise to new product liability claims for the manufacturer. The company could avoid the risks arising from that new liability exposure by discontinuing the manufacture, distribution, and sale of the saw, that is, by applying the avoidance technique to the treatment of that exposure.

Loss prevention techniques try to reduce the *frequency* of a particular loss.

Loss prevention techniques try to reduce the *frequency* of a particular loss. We earlier identified the intersection with the four-way stop signs that Rita must use every day as a hazard that increases the likely frequency of accidents there. A loss prevention technique that Rita could apply is finding an alternate route that is free of intersections with four-way stop signs. Rita's attempt to have a traffic light placed at the intersection was an attempt to apply a loss prevention technique to that hazard, one that requires the cooperation of local government.

Loss reduction techniques try to decrease the *severity* of a particular loss. Rita's use of a seat belt is such a technique. The use of the seat belt will not reduce the *frequency* or *likelihood* of an accident, but it will help to limit the *severity* of any loss that does occur. Rita's new car is probably equipped with at least a driver's side air bag, another loss reduction technique.

> **Loss reduction** techniques try to decrease the *severity* of a particular loss.

Segregation of exposures can be accomplished in two ways—by *separation* or by *duplication*. Separation relies on the dispersal of a particular activity or asset over more than one location. A typical example of separation is for the owners of a clothing manufacturer to store their inventory in several warehouses at different locations. A fire at any one warehouse would not destroy the firm's entire inventory. Separation would not be of much use to Rita. Duplication, on the other hand, relies on having backups, spares, or duplicates of crucial assets readily available. Rita probably keeps a spare tire in the trunk of her car so that if she should find a flat tire early one morning, she could change it immediately. Although she probably does not think of it in these terms, keeping a spare tire in good condition in the trunk of her car is a risk control technique, the segregation of loss exposures achieved through duplication.

> **Segregation of exposures** can be accomplished by *separation* or by *duplication*.

Contractual transfer for risk control means transferring the legal and financial responsibility for a loss arising from the ownership of an asset or from engaging in an activity from one individual or organization to another. This technique would be of little use to Rita. Taking a taxi to work daily would be an expensive and impractical way for her to transfer the legal and financial responsibility for many potential losses arising from her drive to work. She might be able to transfer some of the burden by leasing rather than owning her car. In general, though, Rita is unlikely to be able to transfer the legal and financial responsibility of losses arising from her ownership and use of her car.

> **Contractual transfer for risk control** means transferring the legal and financial responsibility for a loss from one individual or organization to another.

Risk Financing Techniques

We must also consider the risk financing techniques available to Rita. Two types of risk financing techniques can be used—retention and transfer (not to be confused with contractual transfer for risk control).

Retention means that individuals or organizations plan to generate the funds to pay for losses themselves. For organizations, this can amount to a relatively simple accounting transaction or the use of highly sophisticated techniques that have important tax and investment implications. These techniques include current expensing of losses, using an

> **Retention** means that individuals or organizations plan to generate the funds to pay for losses themselves.

unfunded loss reserve, establishing a funded loss reserve, borrowing to pay for losses, establishing a captive insurer, and others.

Rita's retention options are limited to paying for losses out of her savings and earnings or borrowing to pay for losses. Neither of these options is particularly reasonable since we have already determined that Rita could be legally responsible for losses that would more than exhaust all the funds and property that she owns.

> A risk financing **transfer** shifts the financial responsibility for losses from one party to another through a contract.

A risk financing **transfer** shifts the financial responsibility for losses from one party to another through a contract. There are basically two types of risk financing transfers: (1) insurance and (2) noninsurance transfers.

Perhaps the most common type of noninsurance transfer is the use of hold harmless agreements. An organization that uses a contractor to perform particularly hazardous operations, for instance, could use a hold harmless agreement to transfer the responsibility for losses arising from those operations to the contractor. The successful use of such agreements depends in large part on the financial condition of the party that accepts the responsibility for losses and the legal enforceability of the agreement.

Hold harmless agreements are not likely to be of much use to Rita. For instance, a van pool could provide her with an economically feasible alternative to driving to work, and the operators of the van pool could agree to hold passengers harmless for any losses that occur as a result of the commute. But that situation is not probable. The best way for Rita to finance her potential losses is to purchase insurance, although she, like most individuals and organizations, will probably need to use a combination of techniques, both retention and transfer.

> **Insurance** is a system by which a risk is transferred by a person or an organization to an insurance company in exchange for a periodic payment, the insurance premium.

Insurance is a system by which a *risk* is *transferred* by a person or an organization to an insurance company in exchange for a periodic payment, the insurance *premium*. Insurance companies can take these risks because they collect premiums from relatively many individuals and organizations that face the possibility of loss in order to pay for those relatively few losses that actually occur.

The most significant advantage of insurance for Rita and others is that the purchase of insurance enables her to translate the chance of an unknown, difficult-to-predict, and potentially catastrophic financial loss into a relatively small, regular payment. For this reason, the purchase of insurance can give Rita the peace of mind that Chapter 1 described as a benefit of risk management.

Before considering the selection of risk management techniques, review the first two steps in the risk management process—identifying and analyzing loss exposures, and examining the feasibility of alternative risk management techniques—as displayed in Exhibit 2-3.

Exhibit 2-3

First Two Steps in the Risk Management Process

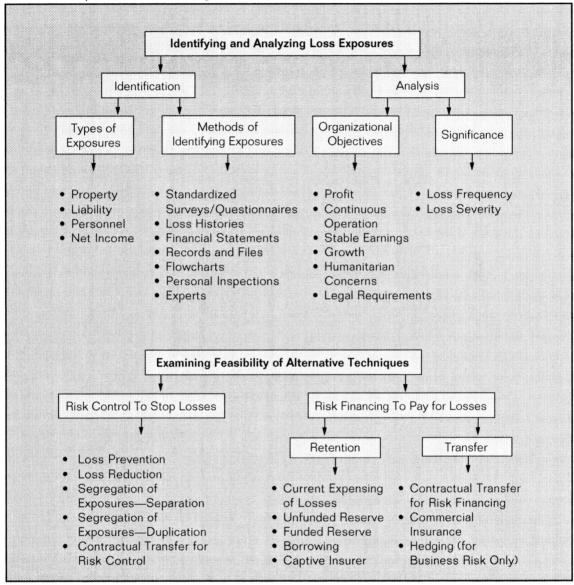

We paid little attention to the "organizational objectives" listed in Exhibit 2-3 because they have less application for Rita than for organizations and will be discussed in later assignments. But we did cover (1) the types of loss exposures, (2) the tools for or methods of identifying loss exposures, (3) the significance of the loss exposures identified, and (4) the risk control or risk financing techniques that are available. We'll consider Rita's objectives when selecting the most appropriate risk management techniques for her in the next section.

Selecting the Most Appropriate Techniques

The risk management process consists of five distinct, sequential steps. The advantage of keeping each of the steps distinct and performing the steps in order is to avoid coming to a decision before all the possibilities have been considered. On the other hand, examining the various techniques available for treating loss exposures is difficult without rejecting some as inappropriate and selecting others. In short, the steps in the risk management process in practice tend to blur and overlap, rather than remaining distinct and sequential.

For instance, when we considered risk control techniques, it quickly became clear that avoidance was not likely to be an appropriate technique for Rita. When we considered risk financing techniques, it quickly became clear that insurance was the only transfer mechanism likely to be appropriate for Rita. It is not necessary to refrain from deciding on appropriate techniques relatively early in the process so long as doing so does not cause important factors to be overlooked or potentially valuable techniques to be ignored.

In order to select the most appropriate techniques, we need to establish some criteria for selection. Risk managers and others who perform the risk management function often use financial criteria in combination with other criteria related to the objectives of the entity, the individual or organization that faces the exposure to loss involved. These other objectives might, for example, be humanitarian or legal in nature.

Rita's basic objective in driving to work is probably simply to get there. But if we had the chance to talk with Rita and could convince her that it might be helpful to think more about her objective, she might eventually agree that her objective is more complicated than that and that she does have some additional considerations in mind. Her objective in driving to work might be stated this way:

> To arrive there on time, safely, with as little trouble as possible, without breaking the law or harming anyone else.

Arriving at work is Rita's basic objective because work is an important element in the way she maintains her standard of living. This is a financial concern and is roughly equivalent to a corporation's objective to survive economically. The other elements of her objective suggest additional criteria—time, safety, and comfort, as well as legal and humanitarian concerns.

The most appropriate risk management techniques with which to treat Rita's exposures are those which support and reinforce rather than conflict with or undermine the achievement of her objective. This sounds obvious, and it is. But the practice of risk management shows that the obvious is too often overlooked. The risk management process is designed to prevent that from happening.

One strength of aligning risk management treatment techniques with individual or organizational objectives is that it helps overcome resistance to implementation of the techniques. If implementing the techniques can help the person or organization achieve its objectives, it is hard to argue against doing so. The risk management process takes people out of the subjective realm of "you should do this because it is good to do" to the objective, businesslike argument of "you should do this because it will help you to achieve what you want to achieve." This strength can be especially important, as we will see in later assignments, when implementation of risk management techniques requires the cooperation of several people at various levels of an organization.

With the criteria for selecting techniques established, we can proceed with developing a mini-risk management program, a series of recommendations, for Rita.

Rita's Mini-Risk Management Program

Selecting appropriate risk management techniques is an attempt to balance two attributes of such techniques: *effectiveness* and *economy*. We said that avoidance was a clearly inappropriate technique for Rita. Why? It would certainly be effective. If Rita stopped driving to work, she would never again be exposed to a chance of loss while doing so. But avoidance would not be economical in the sense that implementing the technique would severely limit if not eliminate Rita's ability to achieve her objective.

Risk managers and others who perform the risk management function must weigh the effectiveness and economy of each technique in the light of the stated objectives that the risk management program is designed to support. To do so, risk managers use forecasts, educated guesses, about (1) the potential financial consequences of loss exposures, (2) the potential effectiveness of various risk control and risk financing techniques, and (3) the potential costs of implementing these techniques. Although the more mathematically precise these forecasts are the more useful they become, we can work with what we discovered when identifying and analyzing Rita's loss exposures and considering the feasibility of the available techniques. Rita's risk management decisions take into account the amount of money she has available to invest in them and the state and other requirements she must meet.

Rita faces four types of loss exposures as a result of her commute—property loss exposures, liability loss exposures, personnel loss exposures, and net income loss exposures. Although some types of exposures are more immediately relevant or readily treated than others, Rita's program should address all four to assure that it is complete and to draw attention to additional risk management efforts that Rita should consider making.

Property Loss Exposures

Rita's car and its contents could be damaged, destroyed, or stolen, with financial consequences for Rita of up to $18,000. The exposure should be treated in the following ways:

Risk Control   Rita should focus on *loss prevention* and *loss reduction* techniques:

General

> Develop and maintain a schedule for routine maintenance and safety inspections of the car

Specific

> Before Leaving Home
> - Allow more time for the drive to work, decreasing the tendency to speed and the irritation experienced at the intersection with four-way stop signs
> - Continue to listen to traffic and weather reports but develop alternate routes to work and become familiar with them. Vary the contents of the trunk to meet weather-related problems based on the season (shovel, scrapers, and salt in the winter, for instance)
>
> Before Leaving Parking Lot
> - Continue quick routine inspection of the vehicle, including tires
> - Continue using the seat belt
> - Double-check that the beverage rack is free of coffee
>
> Local Driving
> - Stay within the speed limit
> - Avoid the intersection with four-way stop signs or strive to reduce the irritation experienced there and continue efforts to have a traffic light installed
>
> Interstate Driving
> - No recommendations
>
> City Driving
> - Be sure speed is sufficiently reduced
>
> Parking at Work
> - Continue to lock car
> - Consider the purchase and use of an antitheft device

Risk Financing   Rita should focus on *insurance* and *retention*:
- Review current insurance coverages with agent
- Consider increasing the amount of the deductible on collision coverage (a deductible is a form of retention) and consider establishing and maintaining a savings or money market account in the amount of the deductible (the equivalent of a funded loss reserve)

Liability Loss Exposures

Rita could be legally responsible for the injury or death of another person or persons or for the damage or destruction of the property of another person or organization, with financial consequences for her in excess of $1 million, a potentially catastrophic loss. The exposure should be treated in the following ways:

Risk Control

See recommendations under "property loss exposures" above

Risk Financing

- Review liability insurance coverages provided by auto insurance with an agent
- Consider increasing the limits of liability (the maximum amount the insurance company will pay for an auto-related liability loss)

Personnel Loss Exposures

Rita could be disabled or killed as the result of an auto accident during her drive to work, diminishing or eliminating her ability to earn a living and to meet her financial obligations or achieve her financial objectives. She should not ignore these exposures, but they raise issues involving all of her assets, obligations, and financial activities beyond the scope of her drive to work. She should treat these exposures by developing a broad personal risk management plan that could address her savings and investments, life insurance, health insurance, retirement planning, estate planning, and so on.

Net Income Loss Exposures

Rita has routine expenses for gas, the maintenance of her car, fees for her driver's license, tags, and registration, her car payments, and her car insurance premiums that must come out of her earnings, or revenues. These expenses could be unexpectedly increased by maintenance problems with the car or fines for traffic violations. The exposure should be treated in the following ways:

Risk Control

1. Driving within the speed limit and otherwise abiding by traffic regulations should reduce if not eliminate the fines for traffic violations (loss prevention and reduction).
2. Maintenance schedules and inspections should decrease the likelihood of major unforeseen expenses for maintenance problems (loss reduction).

Risk Financing

1. Prepare a budget to determine exactly what these expenses are and how best to pay for them (the equivalent to current expensing of losses)
2. Become familiar with the warranty on the car to determine the nature and extent of the financial help available through it (noninsurance transfer)
3. Consider establishing a separate savings or money market account for unforeseen auto-related expenses, perhaps including the increased insurance deductible referred to above (the equivalent of a funded loss reserve)

Reprinted with permission of Insurance Information Institute.

Coordination of Recommendations

Although many of these recommendations appear separate and distinct, they should be combined and coordinated. Insurance premiums can be reduced through discounts offered to those who qualify for them, for instance. Rita probably already receives a discount if her car is equipped with air bags. Her risk control activities should help her to qualify eventually for a safe driver discount if she does not qualify now. Risk control and risk financing techniques are combined in a risk management program so that they are both effective and economical, that is, they are designed to work together to help Rita achieve her objective of getting to work "on time, safely, with as little trouble as possible, without breaking the law or harming others."

Implementing the Chosen Techniques

Rita could implement most of the recommendations of her program quickly and easily. Most of the recommendations would be implemented if she changed some habits and reviewed her auto insurance coverages with an insurance agent. On the other hand, she might decide to plan to purchase and use an additional antitheft device for her car in about a year and look into developing a full personal risk management plan that would include investments and preparing a will.

Exhibit 2-4
The Risk Management Process Is Continuous

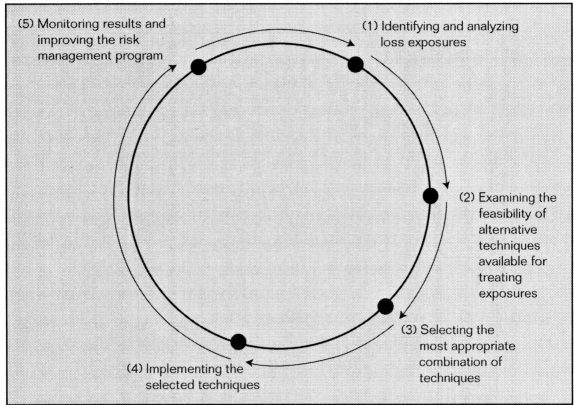

(5) Monitoring results and improving the risk management program

(1) Identifying and analyzing loss exposures

(2) Examining the feasibility of alternative techniques available for treating exposures

(3) Selecting the most appropriate combination of techniques

(4) Implementing the selected techniques

As we will see in later assignments, implementation of risk management techniques can be much more complex and difficult for the risk manager of an organization than it is for Rita.

Monitoring and Improving the Risk Management Program

Risk management programs need to be monitored for several reasons. First, monitoring the program will assure that it does what it was designed to do. Second, loss exposures are dynamic rather than static, that is, they change over time. As Rita's car ages, for instance, its value will decline, a fact that will change the financial consequences for Rita of her property loss exposure. Changes in exposures imply at least the possibility of changes in the most appropriate techniques for treating them. Finally, events can occur that prompt a reevaluation of the risk management program—an accident, for instance, or the purchase of a new car should trigger a new look at the program. A new look at the program requires a new identification and analysis of exposures, the first step in the risk management process. In this way, the risk management process is continuous. (See Exhibit 2-4.)

Rita's monitoring system need not be complex. She might simply keep a copy of her program on a computer disk, make notes on it, indicating which recommendations she has implemented and which she has postponed, and then review it occasionally to see what has been done, the results achieved, and what remains to be done. Once again, this step can be much more complex and difficult in an organizational setting and will be considered in more detail in later chapters.

SUMMARY

Rita's drive to work is a familiar and relatively simple activity. Nonetheless, it introduced you to the steps in the risk management process, the methods and tools used for identifying and analyzing loss exposures, and the techniques available for treating loss exposures. The five steps in the risk management process are:

1. Identifying and analyzing loss exposures

2. Examining the feasibility of alternative techniques

3. Selecting the most appropriate techniques or combination of techniques

4. Implementing the selected techniques

5. Monitoring and improving the risk management program

The methods used to identify and analyze loss exposures include

1. Surveys or questionnaires

2. Financial statements

3. Records and files

4. Flowcharts

5. Personal inspections

6. Consulting experts

In addition, exposures are classified by the four types of loss exposures—property, liability, personnel, and net income.

The chapter also covered the various risk control and risk financing techniques available.

The examples in later chapters might be less familiar and more complex. Still, the steps in the process, the identification methods, and the risk control and risk financing techniques will remain basically the same. Learning these steps, methods, and techniques now will not only help you in the later assignments of this course but will also help you achieve the main aim of this course, which is to help you more thoroughly understand why and how the risk management function is performed.

REVIEW QUESTIONS AND EXERCISES

1. The chart below summarizes the first two steps in the risk management process. Fill in the blanks in the chart.

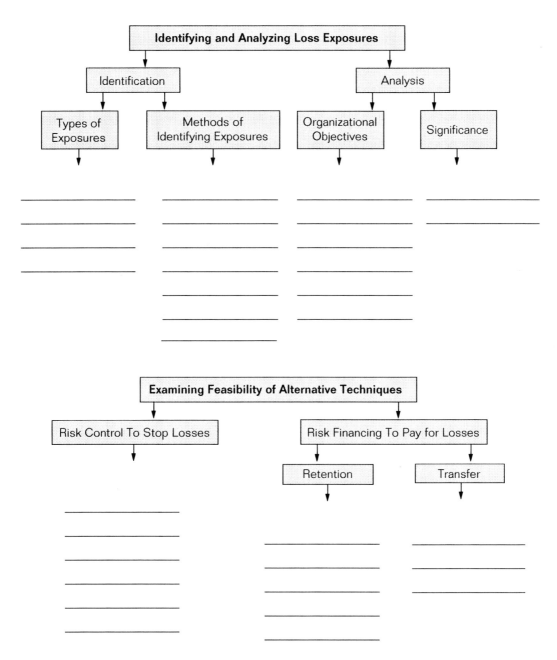

When you have finished, compare your answers with the chart on page 29. If your answers differ from those in the chapter, reread the relevant pages and correct your answers.

2. List the terms you used to fill in the blanks in the chart. Briefly describe or explain each term.

3. Briefly describe the difference between loss frequency and loss severity.

4. The owner of Aquarils, a pet store specializing in tropical fish, noticed a sharp increase in the number of patrons who slipped and fell on the shop's floor in recent months.

    (a) What type(s) of loss exposure does the slipping and falling of patrons potentially represent for the owner of Aquarils?

    (b) If you had to suggest two methods of analyzing this loss exposure, which methods would you choose? Give reasons for your choices.

    (c) Give an example of a hazard that might be related to this exposure.

5. Retention and insurance are both risk financing techniques. How do they differ?

6. Briefly describe the third step in the risk management process.

7. What risk control techniques do you use to treat the loss exposures you face as the result of owning and operating a car?

8. Is using a seat belt a loss prevention or a loss reduction technique? Explain.

9. Briefly explain the difference between the effectiveness and the economy of a risk management technique.

10. A risk management rule of thumb states that each exposure should be treated by at least one risk control technique *and* one risk financing technique. Why?

ANSWERS TO ASSIGNMENT 2 QUESTIONS

1. Summary of the first two steps in the risk management process:

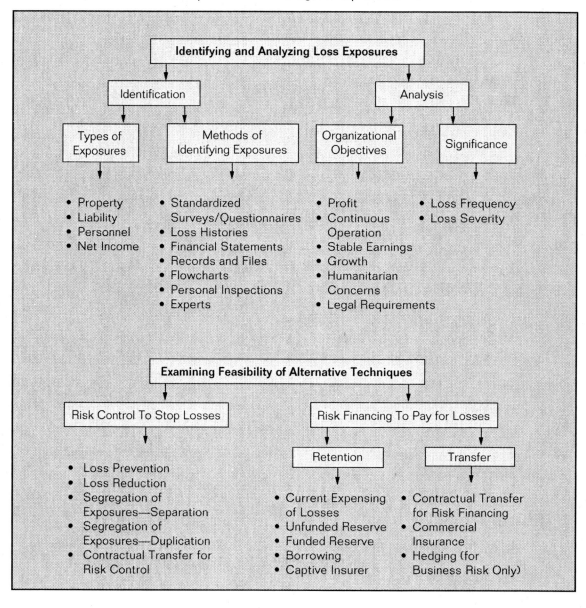

2. (Define the terms listed in the answer to Question 1.)

3. Difference between loss severity and loss frequency:

   - Loss severity is the amount (extent) of damage or injury resulting from losses.

   - Loss frequency is how often losses occur.

4. Aquarils pet store:

   a. Loss exposures because of patrons' slip and fall accidents include liability loss for patrons' injuries and net income loss if people do not patronize the shop because they perceive it to be dangerous.

   b. Two methods of analyzing the loss exposure might include the following:

      - Estimate the potential loss severity and its effect on the organization's ability to continue operations. If severe losses imposed through lawsuits are anticipated, the ability of the organization to continue operations may be in jeopardy.

      - Determine the loss frequency and project that over a specified time period. Increasing loss frequency could also create humanitarian concern for the welfare of patrons.

   c. An example of a hazard that might be related to this exposure is water spilled from the fish tanks onto the shop floor, increasing the likelihood of a loss.

5. Differences between retention and insurance: Insurance is a system in which a person or an organization transfers a risk is to an insurance company in exchange for a periodic payment (premium). Retention involves no transfer of risk. The individual or organization plans to retain the exposure and to pay for the losses.

6. The third step in the risk management process involves selecting the most appropriate risk management techniques. This means establishing criteria for selection, which are usually a combination of financial criteria and other criteria related to the objectives of the organization.

7. Risk control techniques to treat the loss exposures of owning and operating a car include the following: wear seat belts, keep car in good working order, check tires for wear, obey the speed limit and other rules of the road, and drive defensively.

8. Using a seat belt is a loss reduction technique because it reduces the potential severity of a loss.

9. Differences between the effectiveness and the economy of a risk management technique: Effectiveness deals with how successful risk control measures are; economy deals with the price for that effectiveness. A risk management technique that is perfectly successful in controlling the risk may have too high a price. Likewise, an inexpensive technique might not be effective.

10. Each exposure should be treated with at least one risk control and one risk financing technique because, despite the best efforts to prevent or control losses, some losses still can occur. Therefore, having both a risk control and a risk financing technique in place provides more protection.

Assignment 3

BEFORE YOU BEGIN

The first two assignments concentrated on terminology, a basic understanding of the five steps in the risk management process, and how that
process can be used to handle the uncertainty that comes with the
chance of loss—the fundamentals of risk management as a *technical*
activity. In this assignment, the focus shifts to an organizational setting,
and we begin the consideration of risk management as a *management*
activity. Part of this shift in focus means that this assignment will pay
more attention to the last two steps in the risk management process than
Assignment 2 did.

EDUCATIONAL OBJECTIVES FOR ASSIGNMENT 3

After completing this assignment, you should be able to:

1. Describe the fourth and fifth steps of the risk management process.

2. Describe how the risk management process works in an organizational
    setting.

3. Describe some of the ways organizations evaluate their risk management
    programs.

4. Describe the importance of risk management for organizations.

OUTLINE OF REQUIRED READING

I. The Open Door Policy: A Case Study
   A. Evaluation
      1. Implementation
      2. Monitoring
II. Summary

Chapter 3
Risk Management at the Office

Chapter 2 emphasized the "risk" in risk management. This chapter takes a closer look at the "management" aspect of risk management. It begins with a case study—The Open Door Policy—and then evaluates it. The case study and evaluation are designed to help you understand how risk management works in organizations.

THE OPEN DOOR POLICY: A CASE STUDY

Carl Francis, the chief financial officer of Urban University—his official title is treasurer—stood in the den of his house, staring at the TV in disbelief. Paula Unruh, the recently appointed president of Urban, was smiling from the screen and telling an interviewer on the local evening news that she was going to open the university's gym to children who lived in the neighborhood for their use after school: "There's a real need for recreational facilities, and we have this gym...."

Carl shook his head and shouted up the stairs to his wife, "She's a loose canon, I tell you. Journalists hear about what we're going to do before anybody else does. She makes decisions and announcements without discussing things with anyone. This could be big trouble for us."

"It'll be fine," Ellen Francis called down from the kitchen. "Just talk with her about it in the morning. It'll be fine."

"It'll be fine, all right," Carl muttered in disgust as he turned off the television. "It'll be fine when some parent smacks us with a lawsuit because a kid breaks a leg in our gym. . . ."

***

Carl arrived at his office early the next morning and immediately began making phone calls.

His first call was to the president. An administrative assistant said the president would have to return Carl's call. She couldn't say when. His second call was to the Community Affairs office. Carl listened to a recorded voice express interest in his call and urge him to leave a message after the tone. He threw the phone down. His third call was to the Public Relations office. Someone there told him that the president held the TV interview with the intention of talking about a fund-raising effort to build an addition to the science building. Nobody in the Public Relations office knew anything about neighborhood children using the gym. Finally, Carl called the Legal Affairs office. Rita McGoff told Carl that she had seen the president on the news but had not previously heard anything about the plans for the use of the gym. She said she had written a memo alerting her boss to the potential liability problems the plan posed. "Good," Carl told her. "I'm glad somebody around here's trying to stay on top of things."

Carl sat with the palms of his hands on the top of his head, staring out the window. He felt frustrated that he could not take some definite action and briefly wondered whether his frustration was with the new president's surprise decision or with his need to adjust to working with her. He and the recently retired president had worked together for twelve years. They got along well, and Carl felt he had always known where he stood. Now everything seemed up in the air.

He decided to call the university's insurance broker. A new account executive, Igor Buchenzenko, CPCU, ARM, had been assigned to the university. Carl had not yet met him, but he had received a letter from him. This would be a good time to see what kind of service Carl could expect from the new account executive.

Carl dialed the number.

"P and L Insurance. Buchenzenko speaking. How may I help you?"

"Let me count the ways," Carl said and then introduced himself. He told Igor that he learned for the first time the night before while watching the news that the university's president plans to let neighborhood children use the gym after school.

"You weren't just watching TV," Igor said. "You were performing step five in the risk management process."

"I was performing what?" Carl shouted.

"Step five in the risk management process—monitoring and improving your risk management program. Your recognition of the liability exposure posed by the president's announcement gives us a real opportunity to show your new president just what we can do for Urban U. Do you think you could give me an hour or two this afternoon?"

"Sure."

"Good. Three this afternoon all right? At the gym?"

"Wouldn't you rather meet here in my office?"

"No. Let's inspect the gym."

"OK," Carl said. "Three at the gym it is."

After hanging up the phone, Carl was confused; he didn't know exactly what Igor had in mind, but he had to admit he was feeling much better. He turned to other things and caught himself whistling later in the day.

∗∗∗

No one was waiting outside the gym when Carl arrived. The lobby was empty, but the door to the gym was open, and he could hear the bouncing of a basketball.

A short, pudgy man with thick glasses was practicing jump shots. Carl noticed that the man was wearing a crimson-and-gold striped tie—Urban's colors—but had removed his suit jacket. He missed a shot and waved to Carl as he retrieved the ball.

"Carl?" the man asked, coming toward him with his right hand outstretched, the basketball in his left.

"Igor Buchenzenko," he continued without waiting for a reply and shaking Carl's hand. "Nice to meet you. We won't be able to let the school children get away with this," he told Carl, grinning and pointing to his stocking feet. "Footwear's going to be a key, I've learned."

"A key to what?"

"I called the department of recreation. Most of the injuries that arise from this kind of operation, at least as I see it, are twisted ankles and scrapes and bruises from falls, occasionally a broken leg. Improper footwear's a contributing fact—a *hazard*. We need to protect your floor, so no street shoes. But we need to protect the kids, too, so no bare or stocking feet. We're going to have to require gym shoes. But the layout's terrific."

"I'm glad you like it."

"I mean from a traffic control standpoint. Look. I've made a sketch." Igor showed Carl the sketch that appears in Exhibit 3-1.

"We want the kids to enter in an orderly way, and we want to confine them to the gym area. At least, that's what I'd recommend. The lobby gives us a place for them to gather until we're ready to open. We have to consider hours of operation, of course. We keep the inside door locked until opening time. Then we open up, let everybody in, but keep the door to the locker room and the door to the offices and classrooms behind the gym locked."

Exhibit 3-1
Sketch of Urban's Gym

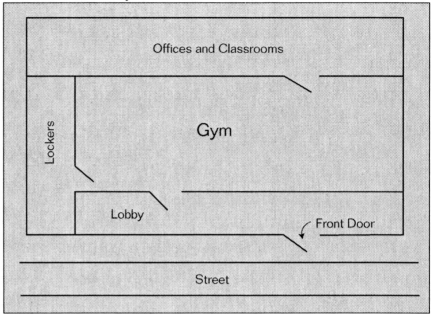

Carl interrupted him. "I'm confused. I thought you were going to tell me how much the premium on our liability insurance was going to go up," Carl told Igor. "I thought when the president heard the price she'd forget about turning the gym over to kids after school. We're a university, not a playground."

"Well, you know best, of course" Igor said, sitting on the floor of the gym and pulling on his loafers. "We can just talk liability insurance if you'd like. But I was hoping I could help you use this idea about the gym as a way to educate the president and maybe some of your other administrative department heads about risk management. The problem you mentioned this morning was that you hadn't been consulted before the decision was announced. I thought if we could help shape the president's policy and help her find a way to implement it without undue risk, she'd see the value in consulting you and working with you in the future."

"I thought you'd give me ammunition I could use to shoot her policy down," Carl said.

"Not sure that would be wise, Carl. New presidents usually don't look favorably on sabotage."

"I didn't think of it that way. I just thought she was going off half-cocked."

"Let's go back to your office and talk it over some more," Igor said, straightening his tie.

✳✳✳

Back at the office, Igor apologized to Carl. "We both made mistakes in our thought processes," he said. "I should have started at the beginning."

"That's all right," Carl said. "I'm having second thoughts about my own position anyway."

"Remember when I said you had been performing the fifth step in the risk management process?"

"Sure."

"Well, we both short-circuited the process, skipped from there to step three—selecting techniques—without performing the first and second steps—identifying the exposures and evaluating risk management techniques. You came up with two techniques—*avoidance*, don't let the kids use the gym, and we'll face no risk of loss as a result of the kids using the gym, and *insurance*, let's get more liability insurance in case a loss arises from this new use of the gym. I came up with an approach based on *risk control*—control the traffic flow, require gym shoes, work on loss prevention and loss reduction. We should have gone back to step one—identifying and analyzing the exposures."

"Good. Let's do that now," Carl said.

"I actually did do that after I spoke with you. Like I said, I called the department of recreation and got some loss data on similar operations, with school-age kids using gyms. I'd been reviewing your insurance coverages recently in preparation for calling for an appointment to introduce myself to you and discuss some ideas I have for the way we should work together in the future. I thought you had plenty of coverage and that this new use for the gym did not represent such a significant shift in the exposure that it should influence your premium. But I called the liability underwriter to confirm that. Urban U. is covered with no increase in premium if you implement the president's policy in a rational way."

"You're kidding."

"No. You've got strong coverage. And a place like this has all kinds of visitors and guests—visiting faculty, lecturers, parents, friends of students, the general public, even the neighborhood kids who walk through the campus on their way home from school all the time. You have good coverage."

"Well, if you're not going to try and sell me more insurance, I'm surprised you've gone to all this trouble."

Igor laughed. "Carl, one of the things I decided when I reviewed your file was to recommend you consider hiring a full-time risk manager. Urban's grown to such an extent and its exposures have become so complex and change so frequently that there's no way you can handle the university's risk management needs as an additional duty. It's unrealistic—unfair to you and to the university. Your phone call simply reinforced what I was already thinking."

"I see."

"This is no criticism of you, Carl. On the contrary, you're responsible for the strong liability coverages that are in place. The fact that you realized the risk management implications of the president's announcement and wanted to deal with them quickly is to your credit and speaks volumes for your dedication to the university."

"What are you suggesting?"

"That you tell the president you want to present her with a plan for implementing her policy on the use of the gym. If she likes the plan, your position with her will be strengthened, the policy can be implemented without undue risk, and that success might demonstrate to the president and others that the university needs a risk manager, somebody to take this approach to *all* of the university's administrative policies."

"Why are you doing all this, Igor?"

"You're my client, Carl, but I'm new to you. It's a logical time for you to ask why you use my services and to wonder if you should continue doing so. If I can help you, with advice and expertise as much as with insurance coverages, my chances of maintaining and strengthening our long-term relationship are increased."

The phone rang. Carl excused himself and answered it. "Hi, Paula. Thanks for returning my call. Do you have a little time tomorrow? I'd like to discuss implementation of the new policy you announced on the news last night." He smiled at Igor. "Two o'clock in your office? Fine, Paula. See you then."

Evaluation

By this point, Carl and Igor have completed the first three steps in the risk management process:

1. Identifying and analyzing exposures to loss

2. Examining the feasibility of alternative risk management techniques

3. Selecting what appears to be the best risk management technique(s)

As Igor pointed out, they did not go through these steps in a sequential way. Instead, they drew different conclusions about how to proceed by first selecting risk management techniques. This kind of abbreviated risk management process frequently occurs in practice, but Igor appropriately drew attention to it and set about correcting it.

In order to eliminate the possibility of overlooking appropriate treatment techniques, Igor used three of the methods for identifying exposures—consultation with experts (the department of recreation and the liability underwriter), a physical inspection, and a rough sketch that served as a kind of flowchart. As a result of these methods, he expanded Carl's concern with the university's liability exposure to also consider a property exposure, potential damage to the floor of the gym. When you read the implementation plan that Carl and Igor present, consider whether it is designed to treat any other types of exposures.

Their examination of the alternative risk management techniques was heavily influenced by Igor's confirmation that the university's current liability insurance would provide coverage with no increase in premium. This knowledge freed Carl and Igor to concentrate on risk control techniques.

Carl and Igor worked late so that Carl would be ready for his meeting with the president the next day. But they found they enjoyed working together and were proud of the results they achieved. By the time he arrived home after work that evening, Carl told his wife he couldn't imagine why he had objected to the president's announcement. "School kids need a place to play and we have a gym. Bringing the two together is the most sensible thing in the world, so long as we can manage the risks that it presents."

The next day, Carl asked the university's president to review the following document he had prepared with Igor:

Plan for Implementing Urban University's Open Door Policy

In order for the university to achieve its goals, it must develop and maintain good relations with the community. One way to develop such relations is President Unruh's policy of opening the gymnasium for use by neighborhood children after school. Although this policy presents us with a real possibility for improving community relations, it poses some risks for the university, the most serious of which is the potential for lawsuits arising from injuries to the children who use our facilities. In order to carry out the policy while managing our risks, the following plan is proposed:

1. *Use of the gym by neighborhood children should be limited to weekdays between 3 P.M. and 5 P.M.*

2. *A security guard should be assigned to the gym during those hours of operation.*

3. *Two to four university student monitors should be hired to work at the gym before, during, and after the hours of operation to prepare for the arrival of the children, supervise play, and see the children safely off the premises.*

4. *All gym equipment other than the baskets and basketballs should be securely stowed away during the hours of operation.*

5. *The doors leading from the gym to the locker room and to the office and classroom area behind the gym should be locked throughout the hours of operation.*

Continued on next page.

6. *The lobby should be unlocked and available for children who arrive before 3 P.M.*

7. *Student monitors should unlock the door to the gym at 3 P.M., greet the children, distribute the basketballs, and check to see that the children abide by the rules of the gym.*

8. *A large sign with the following rules of the gym should be prominently displayed in the lobby:*

    a) *Gym shoes required—no street shoes, no bare feet, no stocking feet.*

    b) *No food or drinks.*

    c) *No smoking.*

    d) *Anyone who breaks the rules will be asked to leave.*

9. *The emergency room of the University Hospital should be notified of the potential for an emergency or a potential increase in patients during the hours of the gym's operations.*

"I like the title, Carl," Paula Unruh told him. "Open Door Policy captures the spirit of what I had in mind. And it's certainly true that we won't be able to achieve our goals if we don't develop better relations with the community. Too little has been done about that, and if relations deteriorate, it could affect our reputation and our ability to attract students and faculty. But the tone of the rest of it is a little forbidding and negative, almost contrary to the spirit of what I had in mind."

"It's an internal document, Paula. I thought the advantages of the policy were clear enough, but I've been worried that too little thought had been given to the potential problems. Open Door Policy is the phrase I think we should use to describe the policy. But let me explain the rationale for the recommendations.

"I met with our insurance broker yesterday and we took a risk management approach to the problem. My main concern when we started, I admit, was the financial well-being of the university."

"There's no need to apologize for that," Paula smiled. "As treasurer, that's an important part of your job. And I'm well aware that I might not think in those terms often enough."

"By the time we were done, my main concern was how to open the gym to kids safely. Our broker had checked with the department of recreation and learned that the most frequent injuries from free play in a gym are broken legs, twisted ankles, and cuts, bruises, and scrapes from falls. The use of inappropriate foot gear is likely to increase the frequency and the severity of such injuries. We can make things safer for the kids, limit our liability exposure, and protect the university's property—the gym floor—simply by requiring gym shoes."

"OK. But what about these brief hours of operation?"

"If we open earlier, we could be encouraging truancy. If we stay open later, we might have worried or angry parents coming to look for their kids. If all goes well and we want to extend the hours later, we can. But it's better to do that than to start with longer hours and have to cut back. Besides, the hours of operation translate into expenses if we think about salaries for the security guard and student monitors."

"I was just coming to that. Why do you recommend them?"

"We'd be asking for trouble and lawsuits if we let the kids play unsupervised. If anyone is hurt, we can see that they are treated quickly. If quarrels or fights erupt, we have people in place who will become aware of the problems and can try to solve them."

"I guess the same thing goes for the other gym equipment."

"Right. We don't want shoulders dislocated on the rings or falls by someone climbing the ropes. Specialized gym equipment should be used under relatively controlled conditions and with a qualified trainer or instructor. We simply want to provide the kids with a place to play."

"You've thought this through, haven't you?"

"I've tried to," Carl said. "But I didn't do it alone. Our insurance broker helped a lot. And if you approve the plan, I'd like to put together a team—with representatives from maintenance, security, community affairs, legal affairs, public relations, and the hospital—that can consider the plan, suggest ways to improve it, and help with its implementation. Successful implementation will require the efforts of a number of departments that don't usually have much contact with each other."

"Yes, I can see that. OK, Carl. You've got my vote."

"Thanks."

"But you can't tackle every new or changing policy in this way, Carl. You wouldn't have the time."

"You're right, Paula. What this whole thing has taught me is that the university could really benefit from a full-time risk manager, somebody who can help shape policies to assure they're implemented in ways that will minimize our risks, our chances of loss. I can't do it; as you said, I don't have the time. Our broker could help much more than in the past by providing services for fees in addition to commissions on insurance sales, but I think we need someone who's familiar with our organization and fully dedicated to it."

"I don't even know exactly what risk managers do," Paula said.

"How about if I do a little research, draw up a job description, and look at where the position should be on our organizational chart? Because of my own background, I also want to be sure the costs of the position will be justified. Once that's finished, we could talk about it again."

"Fair enough," Paula said. "And thanks for your help with the Open Door Policy, Carl. You've turned what was for me a vague idea, little more than a wish, into a practical action plan. I appreciate that."

A month later, Carl was in his den watching the evening news. The president of Urban University was being interviewed in the university's gym. In the background, kids were playing basketball, sitting in groups on the floor doing homework, or just running around. A security guard passed in front of the camera. "We've made the news again," Carl called up the stairs to his wife, while the president explained the university's new Open Door Policy.

Implementation

Step four in the risk management process, implementing the chosen risk management techniques, requires two types of activities, **technical** and **managerial**. Technical activities are related directly to the risk management function and can be carried out by the person or department that performs that function in an organization. Purchasing insurance is an example of a technical activity. Managerial activities, on the other hand, require the cooperation of other managers. Implementing the decision to install sprinklers in the production-line area of a manufacturing firm to reduce the severity of losses caused by fire, for instance, is a managerial activity. The person who performs the risk management function must enlist the cooperation of others to deal with purchasing decisions, personnel decisions, production decisions, scheduling decisions, maintenance decisions, and potentially others.

> **Technical** activities are related directly to the risk management function and can be carried out by the person or department that performs that function in an organization. **Managerial** activities require the cooperation of other managers.

The responsibility for both of these types of activities typically rests with one person or department. In that case, the person or department performing the risk management function is said to have two types of authority—line authority and staff authority. **Line authority** grants the person or department the power to do specific things or to authorize others to do them. Line authority allows risk managers to conduct the technical activities required to implement the chosen risk management techniques. **Staff authority** limits the person's or department's power to giving advice to others about specific things. Risk managers need staff authority to conduct the managerial activities required to implement the chosen risk management techniques.

> **Line authority** grants the person or department the power to do specific things or to authorize others to do them. **Staff authority** limits the person's or department's power to giving advice to others.

Let's use this traditional approach to implementing risk management techniques to evaluate the Open Door Policy case study. Who has the responsibility for the technical and managerial activities required to implement risk management techniques at Urban University? Clearly, Carl Francis does. He purchases insurance for Urban, one of the technical activities required. He also advises the president of the university and can obtain from her the authority to form a team of representatives from several departments. Carl's role on that team can be described as advisory. In short, Carl has line authority to carry out technical activities and staff authority to advise others on managerial matters.

But what about Igor's role? He is the one most responsible for the implementation of the chosen risk management techniques, but he has no authority, either line or staff, at Urban University.

Just as Carl's perspective at the beginning of the case study was too narrow and needed to be broadened to become a risk management perspective, the traditional management perspective is too narrow to allow us to evaluate accurately what occurred in the case. The traditional approach to management issues, with its emphasis on clearly defined areas of responsibility and authority within the organization, and with authority moving from the top of the organization down through layers of managers and supervisors, no longer describes or supports the actual operations of many contemporary organizations.

Let's look at the implementation of chosen risk management techniques at Urban University again, not as a series of decisions made by the person with the appropriate kind of authority, but in a broader context as part of a series of negotiations between suppliers and customers. **Suppliers** are people or organizations who provide products, information, or services to others. **Customers** are the recipients of products, information, or services. Suppliers and customers can be within an organization or outside of it. Suppliers can also be customers when they receive the products, information, or services of others. Similarly, customers become suppliers when they provide products, information, or services to others. The role of people or organizations at any given time is defined by what they are doing at that time—providing or receiving.

> **Suppliers** are people or organizations who provide products, information, or services to others. **Customers** are the recipients of products, information, or services.

A chart of these negotiations in the Open Door Policy case should help make these terms and their meaning clear (see Exhibit 3-2).

Paula Unruh initiated the series of negotiations by indirectly supplying information to Carl Francis. The negotiations temporarily broke down then. Why?

Carl's reaction to, that is, his immediate rejection of Paula's information means that Paula failed to meet Carl's expectations. She did not see Carl as a "customer" for her information, with a set of expectations that she could have taken into account and tried to at least meet, if not exceed. Paula's "failure" was inadvertent. But you can imagine how differently the case study might have gone if it had begun with Paula discussing her planned use of the gym with Carl and asking for his advice about how to implement her plan.

Exhibit 3-2

Negotiations

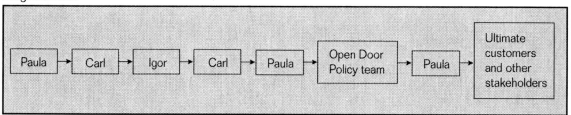

Carl, a "dissatisfied customer" of Paula's, then called Igor and supplied him with information that clearly identified Carl as a customer of Igor's with a set of expectations. Igor rapidly set about trying to exceed Carl's expectations and eventually did so, primarily by showing Carl that the risk management process was a tool with which Carl could solve his problem. Carl was at first confused and disappointed because what Igor supplied was not what Carl had expected. But in time, Carl's expectations were exceeded. Igor's use of the risk management process brought objectivity to the problem, required the use of data as the basis for decisions, and helped to eliminate the emotional and political elements of the problem. One result of Igor's negotiations with Carl was that Carl came to see Paula as a customer for an implementation plan that Carl could supply. With Igor's advice and encouragement, Carl understood how he might exceed Paula's expectations.

Paula was initially confused and disappointed by the plan Carl supplied. But her negotiations with Carl led to her expectations being exceeded, too. Her approval both of the plan and of Carl's recommendation that an interdepartmental team be formed is the clearest sign of this result.

Finally, Paula again became a supplier of information to a large number of relevant "customers" for the university—customers in the broadest sense of groups of people with a real, although not necessarily financial, interest in the organization: the university's Board of Trustees; foundations that award grants to educational organizations; government agencies with an interest in higher education; alumni; students; faculty; members of the neighboring community; parents of students; prospective students; and others. Paula's aim in supplying this information can be described as to exceed the expectations of members of the neighboring community in order to continue to at least meet the expectations of the other groups of customers and stakeholders, interested parties.

There are several advantages to looking at the implementation of risk management techniques in this way. First, Igor is no longer missing from the picture. Second, Paula's ultimate customers also are no longer missing. Our perspective has broadened to include not only Urban's staff—those people who would appear on the university's organizational chart—but also external suppliers (Igor Buchenzenko) and external "customers" (the community, prospective students, and so on). Third, this approach allows us to look at exactly what happened and possibly learn from it.

This approach can also help in the evaluation of step five of the risk management process—the step Carl took without realizing he was doing so, monitoring the risk management program.

Monitoring

There are two primary reasons for monitoring a risk management program. First, monitoring allows risk managers to become aware of changes in exposures or in the availability and cost of alternate risk management techniques. Risk managers should consider adjustments to the program in light of these changes, basically by going through the steps in the risk management process again, if in a more limited way. Second, monitoring allows risk managers to evaluate the results achieved by the program in order to demonstrate to others in the organization the value of the risk management function and of the person or department that performs the function. We'll consider only the first of these reasons now. The second will be discussed in the next chapter.

Igor described Carl's realization that Paula's announcement represented a change in Urban's liability exposures as "performing step five in the risk management process," and it certainly is an incidental kind of monitoring. It would be preferable, though, for Urban to take a systematic approach to this and other aspects of risk management. For this reason, Igor suggested that Urban assign the responsibility for risk management to a full-time employee of the university.

Carl probably had some kind of a systematic approach to monitoring in place. Renewals of insurance policies would trigger a reevaluation and reconsideration of exposures—their values, perils, hazards, and potential financial consequences for the university—by Carl and the insurance broker. That would be the time to increase the amounts of coverage to track with increasing property values, for instance, or to retain more of a risk by accepting higher deductibles. The occurrence of a loss would also trigger such a reevaluation and reconsideration. Several small fires in dormitories might lead an insurance company underwriter to recommend or require the installation of an improved fire alarm system, for example. But Urban lacks a focal point for risk management information. Instead, it has an insurance program combined with uncoordinated risk control techniques implemented by various departments, such as Legal Affairs, Maintenance, and Security.

The Open Door Policy case would have been very different if Carl had a monitoring system for gathering and analyzing risk management information. As treasurer of the university, he already collects a good deal of this information when he prepares the university's annual budget. The heads of various departments are asked to project various costs and expenses based on what they plan to do in the upcoming fiscal year. A review of these projections from a risk management standpoint—looking for changes in exposures, potential new exposures, or alternate ways of treating exposures—would have been one way for Carl to combine a system for monitoring the university's risk management program with his other responsibilities as treasurer.

Such a system would not necessarily have prevented the new university president from announcing her plan for the use of the gym without first considering the risk management implications of the plan. But if Paula Unruh should have thought of Carl as a "customer" for her plan, Carl should have been routinely and systematically seeking, collecting, and analyzing risk management information. If the president heard from Carl with some regularity about his need to know her plans and intentions, she would have been more likely to consult him before making announcements to the public.

The advantage of the situation described in the case study is that the people involved learned how to improve the university's approach to risk management for the future and began taking steps to do so. As Igor realized, the absence of a monitoring system at Urban University was merely symptomatic of the absence of a risk manager and a risk management program. In the next chapter, he will help Carl to change that situation.

SUMMARY

The risk management function is not necessarily performed by an employee of an organization. As the case study showed, an insurance broker or consultant can perform many of the technical and managerial activities usually performed by a risk manager or a risk management department. One weakness with this approach is that the person making the decisions and recommendations has no authority for implementing them and must work through someone who is an employee of the organization. Usually, the risk manager or the risk management department has line authority to carry out technical risk management activities and staff authority to advise others on the managerial activities needed to implement risk management techniques.

If the implementation of risk management techniques is seen in the broader context of negotiations between "suppliers" and "customers," its effects on those outside the organization—an insurance broker, for example, as well as the organization's ultimate customers and stakeholders—become clear.

Monitoring and improving the risk management program, the fifth step in the risk management process, are among the managerial activities risk managers engage in. Risk management programs are monitored for three primary reasons: (1) to identify changes that require adjustments to the program, (2) to continuously improve the program, and (3) to demonstrate to others in the organization the value of the program. Many of the methods or tools used to identify and analyze exposures can also help to monitor the program. Monitoring requires a system for collecting and analyzing risk management information.

REVIEW QUESTIONS AND EXERCISES

1. Define or describe each of the words and phrases listed below:

   (a) Technical risk management activities

   (b) Managerial risk management activities

   (c) Line authority

   (d) Staff authority

   (e) Suppliers

   (f) Customers

2. Describe the fourth step in the risk management process.

3. Describe the fifth step in the risk management process.

4. In the case study, which technical risk management activities did Igor Buchenzenko perform?

5. In the case study, which managerial risk management activities did Carl Francis perform?

6. Describe the relationship between insurance and risk management.

7. Describe two methods or tools used for exposure identification and analysis in the case study.

8. Carl was originally concerned with Urban's liability exposure. Based on your analysis of the plan submitted to Paula Unruh, what other types of exposures are to be treated?

9. A rule of thumb used by many risk managers recommends that each exposure be treated with at least one risk control technique and at least one risk financing technique. Identify one of each type of technique that Urban chose to use to treat the liability exposure arising from the use of the gym by children after school.

ANSWERS TO ASSIGNMENT 3 QUESTIONS

1. (Define key terms)

2. The fourth step in the risk management process involves implementing the chosen risk management technique. This requires two types of activities, technical and managerial. Technical activities are directly related to the risk management function and can be implemented by those who are responsible for the risk management function. Managerial activities require the cooperation of managers.

3. The fifth step in the risk management process is monitoring and improving the risk management program. Risk management programs are monitored for three primary reasons: (1) to identify changes, (2) to continuously improve the program, and (3) to demonstrate to others the value of the program.

4. Igor Buchenzenko performed the following technical risk management activities:

    •   Identified and analyzed loss exposures. For example, he consulted with experts; he visited the university for a physical inspection; and he drew a rough sketch of the gym that served as a flow chart.

    •   Examined the feasibility of alternative risk management techniques by reviewing Urban U.'s insurance file and verifying with the liability underwriters that an increase in coverage was not necessary.

    •   Recommended what appeared to be the best risk management technique: risk control.

5. Carl Francis, along with Igor, worked on an implementation plan and policies that would manage and control the potential risks to Urban U. Mr. Francis presented the plan to the university president and recommended steps to control the risks, such as limiting the time and days the gym would be open, employing a security guard and student monitors, and prohibiting food and drink into the gym.

6. Relationship between insurance and risk management: Insurance is a risk financing technique that transfers a risk from an individual or organization to an insurance company. Risk financing is one component in the second step in the risk management process, that is, examining the feasibility of alternative risk management techniques.

7. Two methods or tools used for exposure identification and analysis in the case study are on-site physical inspection and consulting with experts.

8. Other types of exposures to be treated in the plan submitted to Paula Unruh include the following property exposures—potential damage to the gym floor; to the locker room, offices, and classrooms; and to gym equipment.

9. Urban chose the following techniques to treat the liability exposure arising from the use of the gym by children after school:

    •   Risk Control Technique: Assign an employee who is appropriately trained to monitor the activities of the children in the gym.

    •   Risk Financing Technique: Obtain liability insurance to cover this exposure.

Assignment 4

BEFORE YOU BEGIN

Now that you have learned some basic terminology, have gained a familiarity with the steps in the risk management process, and have a sense of some of the issues raised by trying to implement that process in an organization, we can look at the risk manager in relation to the organization that employs the risk manager. There is no one, single, right relationship between the risk manager and the organization. That relationship will vary based on the nature and goals of the organization and the experience, knowledge, and skills of the risk manager. In this assignment, Carl Francis will do some research, develop objectives and a job description for a risk manager for Urban University, and fill the position.

EDUCATIONAL OBJECTIVES FOR ASSIGNMENT 4

After completing Assignment 4, you should be able to:

1. Explain the relationship between the risk manager and the organization.

2. Describe an organization's risk management objectives and the bases for determining them.

3. Describe some of the activities performed by risk managers in organizational settings and the skills required to perform those activities.

4. Describe methods for measuring risk management results and for evaluating the performance of risk managers.

OUTLINE OF REQUIRED READING

Chapter 4

The Risk Manager and the Organization

Any organization that decides to establish a full-time position dedicated to risk management faces many questions: What will the risk manager do? To whom should the risk manager report? Can the position be justified on financial or other grounds? Considering these questions should help you better understand the relationship between the risk manager and the organization that employs the risk manager, some of the characteristics of successful risk managers, and the financial and other benefits of risk management for organizations.

Carl Francis had to answer these questions after he promised Paula Unruh that he would do some research, draw up a job description, establish where the new position would fit on the university's organizational chart, and determine that the position could be justified financially. He might have underestimated what would be required to answer these questions, but Igor Buchenzenko put him on the right track by having Carl contact another one of Igor's clients, Victoria Perez, ARM, the director of risk management for a large chemical manufacturer, Bryan International Group.

A VISIT

"I feel like a stranger in a strange land," Carl told Victoria Perez as she led him back to her office after a brief tour of one of Bryan's manufacturing plants. "Your operation is so different from ours."

"I guess that's why Igor suggested you visit," Victoria said. "The way we are organized certainly will not work for the university. But learning how we're organized should give you some ideas about how to set up the university's risk management program."

They sat at a table in Victoria's office. She had placed documents on the table for them to review while they talked.

"Let me give you a little background first," Victoria began. "Then we'll look at a few documents. I have copies for you that you can take with you for reference."

"Thanks."

"I'm glad to help. I've been through much of what you're going through. I wasn't born a risk manager," she laughed. "I started my career as a commercial lines underwriter with an insurance company in town. I eventually specialized in HPRs."

"HPRs? Even the language is strange here."

"Highly protected risks," Victoria explained. "HPRs are organizations that, through the use of loss control techniques, become better-than-average risks for their class. I found that I was more interested in inspecting industrial facilities and developing loss reduction recommendations than I was in underwriting the business. I joined Bryan International as an insurance buyer years ago—more years than I care to mention," she laughed again.

"So you weren't a risk manager from the start here?"

"No. My experience as an underwriter helped me to communicate with brokers and insurance companies and helped me to understand what they needed and why they needed it. At the same time, I inspected our own facilities and made loss prevention recommendations that sometimes went beyond what the underwriters required. As I said, risk control techniques have played a big part in handling industrial risks for a long time, even back into the nineteenth century. Long ago Standard Oil replaced lawn mowers with goats at a refinery in New Jersey. The goats kept the grass trimmed without giving off dangerous sparks."

"So the risk control aspects of risk management go way back," Carl said.

"Right. What moved us from a combination of insurance with relatively modest retentions and risk control to a more aggressive program for managing risks were two things that happened almost simultaneously. First, competition increased and we began to lose market share. As a result, we started a global continuous improvement effort, a new way of aligning our group of companies so that we would stay focused on the needs of our customers and could find a way to judge our results in measurable terms. We wanted to measure the results on a basis that would include but not be limited to the bottom line, our short-term financial results. Second, we ran into difficulty obtaining product liability insurance at any price."

"What did you do?"

"The short answer is that we formed a **captive insurance company** to write the coverage for our product

A **captive insurance company** is a risk financing technique, an insurance company established as a subsidiary of an organization to provide that organization with insurance.

exposures. The slightly longer answer is that we broadened our perspective to a risk management perspective. Applying the risk management process to our operations made us realize that our assets would permit us to retain more of our exposures than we had in the past and with a number of benefits—tax advantages, a stronger cash position, and measurable contributions to our bottom line."

"But Urban's a nonprofit."

"Sure. But you want to survive, perhaps even grow, and you want to use your resources and manage your risks as efficiently as possible. To do that you have to generate revenues that exceed your expenses. As I said, what we do will not necessarily work for you, but it might help you to see what you should do. I'm not urging you to start a captive, either, although the time might come when Urban will join with other universities to form one or when Urban will participate in some other alternatives to commercial insurance. The point I want to make is that your risk management program should have some specific objectives, objectives that are tied into the organization's goals and reflect the organization's situation."

"OK."

"That's how we came to establish a Risk Management Department. I went from an insurance buyer who made risk control recommendations to a risk manager. We now have nine people in the department."

"That seems like a lot."

"Five professionals in addition to me and three administrative assistants. Have a look at our department's organizational chart." (See Exhibit 4-1.)

"What do all these people do?"

"Well, as I said, we manage highly protected risks. Loss prevention and reduction are crucial for any organization that's involved in an industry that's as hazardous as the manufacture and distribution of chemicals are. We devote a full-time manager to property loss prevention. Our liability exposures are also potentially catastrophic. We run our captive insurance company, negotiate reinsurance, and oversee the payment of claims, in addition to purchasing commercial insurance. Our manager of corporate risk management heads up those operations and is supported by an assistant manager and our claim administrator. You have to remember that we're a group of companies with operations worldwide. I'm sometimes surprised that we can manage with so few people in the department, and we still rely heavily on brokers, insurance companies, outside claim adjusters, loss control specialists, and other consultants."

"You're running a business within a business."

"Exactly. Our newest position is that of our computer technology manager. Bryan International has a corporate objective of making the most of automation, computers, and new technologies generally. Nobody in the department is a specialist in that area. This new position is slowly but surely reorganizing our department and the way we work."

Exhibit 4-1

Organizational Chart—Corporate Risk Management

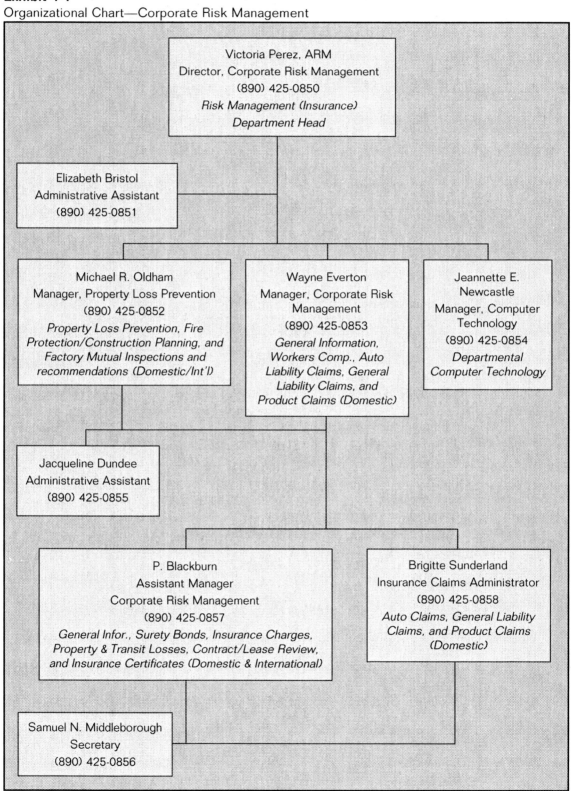

"You say this emphasis on technology is the department's contribution to the achievement of a corporate goal. But how do you determine that?"

"Each of our departments develops what we call a vision statement, some people use other terms, phrased in such a way that it is a clear subset of Bryan International's vision statement. Read ours." (See Exhibit 4-2.)

Exhibit 4-2
Risk Management Department Vision Statement

TO PROVIDE A WORLD-CLASS RESOURCE TO THE BRYAN INTERNATIONAL GROUP TO ASSIST THEM IN MANAGING THEIR CONTROLLABLE LOSS THROUGH THE DEVELOPMENT OF RISK AND INSURANCE MANAGEMENT PROGRAMS.
Why:
TO MAKE A POSITIVE CONTRIBUTION TO THE COMPANY'S NET INCOME THROUGH MINIMIZING COST OF RISK AND ITS FLUCTUATION, AND PROTECTING OUR CASH POSITION.

"It doesn't say anything about computers."

"Right. The vision statement is broad and general. For more specific guidance, we translate it into what we call 'Initiatives,' a list of areas we want to emphasize. Here's the list." (See Exhibit 4-3.)

Exhibit 4-3
Risk Management Initiatives

Practice the Bryan International Group Process Quality Management model

Revolutionize the way we operate through computer technology

Eliminate non-value added activities

Meet customer requirements through timely delivery of high quality products/services

Initiate/bring leading edge technology to our customers

Understand our customers and their expectations/requirements

Measure/benchmark

"I see you have technology listed here twice."

"More often than that, really. The two direct references mean we'll use it in two ways. First, technology should help us streamline our own operations. Second, we want to use technology to help streamline the risk management operations of our customers."

"You do risk management for your customers?"

"Yes. Not Bryan's customers. Our *internal* customers. The managers of that plant we just toured are among our biggest customers. But we have eight companies with twenty-three locations worldwide making up the Bryan International Group. They're all our customers, and we want to make their record keeping and other functions as efficient as possible through an appropriate use of technology."

"You suggested there are indirect references to technology in these initiatives."

"Yes. It plays a part in all of them, of course, but especially the elimination of non-value added activities and assuring timely deliveries of products and services."

"I can see that. But this seems far afield from risk management."

"'Seems' is the right word. If we don't conduct ourselves in ways that fit Bryan's culture, we'll lose credibility fast, antagonize and disappoint our customers, and introduce doubts about the value of risk management for Bryan."

"So the moral of the story is to design a risk management program that's attuned to an organization's culture, whether bottom-line oriented or non-profit, whether a highly hazardous industry or a university campus, and also aligned with its goals."

"I'd say so. We have whole loose-leaf notebooks full of departmental procedures and guidelines, but I just want to show you one more document, our statement of departmental activities." (See Exhibit 4-4.)

Exhibit 4-4
Statement of Departmental Activities

Identifying loss exposures in all areas of business

Measuring (evaluating) identified exposures in financial terms

Eliminating/reducing exposure to accidental damage to property or injury to people

Recommending, implementing, and managing appropriate risk financing mechanisms

Selecting and managing quality-based external partnerships

Enjoying our work (earning our pay)

"Now it looks like we're back to risk management," Carl said.

"I don't think we ever left it. We can't separate the technical aspects of the function from the managerial aspects. Performing these activities would be inefficient, or impossible, or futile without the vision statement to give us direction and without the initiatives to give us guidance. They work together. They allow us to explain to our internal customers why we do what we do in terms they can appreciate, in terms of helping them achieve their objectives. But what I especially wanted to draw your attention to is the next-to-last activity."

"Selecting and managing quality-based external partnerships?"

"Right. We used to select insurance brokers and other consultants on the basis of price alone, or, rather, price and a subjective sense of a comfort level with an individual. But prices and individuals change in time, as we learned years ago. We now have specific quality-based criteria, in terms of automated capabilities, access to markets, types of information and reports supplied, turnaround time, and so on. This emphasis, like the one on technology, represents a group-wide operational method for Bryan International, but it also relates to our departmental vision statement. We're not likely to provide our customers with a 'world-class resource' if we lack quality criteria for supplier selection."

"So even though you're a for-profit corporation and your department is committed to contributing to the organization's net income, you don't buy insurance and other services on the basis of price alone."

"Right. But again, I'm not saying Urban should necessarily take the same approach. What I am saying is that selecting and managing agents, brokers, consultants, and other suppliers will be an important part of your risk manager's job. And that criteria similar to those can help you evaluate that risk manager's performance. Still feel like a stranger in a strange land?"

"No," Carl admitted, shaking his head. "More like a visitor to a strange land who is beginning to pick up the language."

"Well, feel free to visit again, any time, or have your risk manager call me when you hire one. I'd just give you two more pieces of advice, Carl. First, hire someone who's able and willing to learn. That might be the most important attribute for success in risk management these days. And second, have your new risk manager become involved professionally. Join RIMS, the Risk and Insurance Management Society, for instance. Attending meetings and seminars and getting to know other risk managers, people to turn to for advice, might make all the difference."

"Sounds like good advice, Victoria. Thanks. And thanks for the tour and the information. It's given me a lot to think about."

OBJECTIVES, ACTIVITIES, AND RESULTS

Carl's conversation with Victoria and his review of the documents she had given him led him to concentrate on risk management objectives, activities, and results.

Objectives

An organization's risk management objectives often arise from the consideration of an idea that appears in the vision statement of the risk management department of Bryan International Group, the cost of risk.

Organizations experience costs of risk through exposures to loss, whether a loss actually occurs or not.

The cost of risk management represents the resources devoted to managing accidental losses.

Costs of risk are of three types: first, the lives, property, income, or other things of value damaged or destroyed in accidents; second, the loss of potential profits or benefits that could have been gained through the ownership of assets or participation in activities that were avoided as too risky; and third, the resources devoted to managing accidental losses that could have been employed otherwise. The third of these types of costs of risk—the resources devoted to managing accidental losses—represents **the cost of risk management**. The *reduction* of the first two types of costs—actual losses and lost opportunities—represents **the benefits of risk management**. Risk management programs are designed to minimize all three types of costs of risk, the total cost of risk for an organization.

The benefits of risk management are reductions in actual losses and in lost opportunities.

Risk managers often translate these efforts to minimize the three types of costs of risk into objectives that support organizational goals and objectives. Risk management programs are intended to achieve objectives that have value for organizations whether a loss actually occurs or not. As a result, both pre-loss objectives (objectives that are valuable even if no loss occurs) and post-loss objectives (objectives that are valuable after a loss) are established.

Pre-loss objectives have value whether or not a loss occurs.

Examples of **pre-loss objectives** include economy of operations, tolerable uncertainty, legality, and humanitarian conduct. These objectives have value whether or not a loss occurs. Organizations benefit from keeping costs down and allowing managers to make decisions under conditions of tolerable uncertainty at all times. Examples of **post-loss objectives** include survival, continuity of operations, profitability, stability of earnings, growth, and humanitarian conduct. Humanitarian conduct appears in both sets of objectives because no organization operates in isolation. Losses or potential losses influence an organization's behavior, and that behavior influences a broader community outside the organization and the economy in general. An organization's reputation and ultimate success often depend on its sense of social responsibility and its concern for a variety of stakeholders.

In general, the more ambitious an objective is, the more costly it will be to achieve. The senior managers of an organization should help determine and prioritize the organization's risk management objectives. Survival, for instance, might seem to be an exceedingly modest objective. But when you consider that *post-loss objectives include the worst condition an organization's senior management can accept after the most severe foreseeable loss*, it appears much less modest. Many organizations are forced to permanently discontinue

Post-loss objectives include the worst condition an organization's senior management can accept following the most severe foreseeable loss.

operations after a major loss. On the other hand, post-loss objectives can also include simply paying claims promptly and minimizing unnecessary lawsuits.

Carl thought that the risk management function at Urban should use survival as a post-loss objective (the university had experienced temporary interruptions in its activities in the past and had weathered those) and pursue a combination of four pre-loss objectives: economy of operations, tolerable uncertainty, legality, and humanitarian conduct.

Activities

The steps in the risk management process describe in general terms the primary activities to be performed by the risk manager. As we have seen, these include technical and managerial activities, and line and staff activities. Carl wanted to describe these activities briefly and in terms that would reflect the university's culture. He also remembered that his original goal was to establish a focal point for risk management information at the university. He decided to express the activities this way:

- **C**oordinate a risk management program for the university

- **A**dvocate the use of risk management techniques throughout the university

- **R**educe the university's overall costs of risk

- **E**valuate the university's risk management performance

Results

Carl considered several methods for measuring the results of the university's risk management program and evaluating the performance of the risk manager.

First, he thought that a comparison of the university's loss experience from year to year could be used to demonstrate results. If losses went down, the program could be considered a success. If losses went up, the program would need improvement. The problem with this approach, as Carl knew from his familiarity with the university's insurance program, is that luck plays a part in loss experience. It would be as unfair to credit the program with a reduction in losses as it would be to blame the program for an increase in losses, especially if a relatively short period of time, such as one year, was to serve as the basis for comparison.

Second, he thought that the costs of risk management could be shown in comparison with the benefits of risk management, a typical cost/benefit analysis of the program. One difficulty with this approach is that although the costs of risk management—the salary and benefits of the risk manager, a share of overhead, the insurance premiums paid, the costs of installing an alarm system, and so on—are readily translated into dollar figures, some of the benefits are not. How do you measure the value of making a gym available to school children, for example, even if doing so helps to improve the university's relations with the community and supports the university's objective of conducting itself in a humanitarian way? What is the dollar value of the university's president, deans, and department heads making decisions without being paralyzed by intolerable uncertainty?

Third, he thought of evaluating the risk manager's performance based on specific activities to be accomplished within a given time period, for example the number of surveys, interviews, and inspections conducted. The problem with this approach is that it emphasizes and measures activity apart from results, possibly encouraging inefficient and ineffective activities.

Carl thought that he might alleviate some of the problems with these approaches by combining them. He also wanted to discuss the problem with Igor Buchenzenko and perhaps learn what other universities with risk management programs do. He thought the solicitation of regular feedback from the university's senior managers and department heads—the "customers," as Victoria Perez put it, for the risk manager's services—might be the best way to evaluate the performance of the risk manager or the risk management program. That would help emphasize the interdepartmental nature of the function no matter where it appeared on the university's organizational chart.

DUTIES, SKILLS, AND THE ORGANIZATIONAL CHART

Carl decided he was ready to draw up a job description and a statement of the requirements for the position of Urban University's risk manager. His first draft appears in Exhibit 4-5.

Exhibit 4-5
Job Description and Requirements

Title: Risk Manager
Duties: The primary responsibility of the risk manager is to develop and maintain a comprehensive risk management program for Urban University by:
- identifying and analyzing all of those situations that could lead to the university's suffering accidental losses;
- recommending ways to reduce or prevent accidental losses;
- working with other university personnel to implement loss prevention and reduction recommendations;
- recommending ways, in addition to insurance, to offset the financial consequences of accidental losses;
- negotiating the purchase of all insurance for the university;
- serving as a liaison to the Legal Affairs department on claims against the university;

- serving on the committee responsible for the university's Emergency Operations Plan; and
- supervising one administrative assistant.

Requirements: The successful candidate for this position should:
- hold a bachelor's degree in Business or a related field or the equivalent;
- be thoroughly familiar with the university's mission and organization;
- display excellent communication skills;
- be willing to pursue formal education in risk management and insurance;
- have a job history of 3-5 years experience in administrative or managerial positions; and
- have experience in insurance, risk management, finance, or law.

Rereading what he had written, Carl realized he had already decided where the new position should fit on the organizational chart. The new risk manager would be part of the Treasurer's Office and report to him. He made an appointment with Igor Buchenzenko to discuss his plans before presenting them to the president for approval.

Fine Tuning

Carl and Igor stood in the lobby of the gym, eating hot dogs, drinking sodas, and watching a pick-up basketball game. A student monitor ran toward them, shouting, "No food or drinks in here. Can't you read the sign?" They raised their hands in a gesture of surrender, laughed, and backed out of the lobby into the street.

"What did you think of the job description and other statements I faxed you?"

"You've learned a lot. Come a long way in a short time...."

"But...."

"You've surprised me, that's all, in two ways. A pleasant surprise and a not-so-pleasant surprise."

"Tell me the pleasant one first."

"I was pleasantly surprised you're recommending that the risk manager report to you. I thought you might shy away from that, but that makes the most sense."

"I think that will work for now. In time, the function might grow to be a department of its own. Small but independent, like the Community Affairs department. But insurance is such an important part of our program and financial records will be so important for exposure identification and analysis, I'm going to have to be involved for a while anyway. And at this point I know what I want to see happen and no one else does. What's the unpleasant surprise?"

"That you don't want to hire a risk management professional and that you severely limit the role of whoever you will hire, by insisting that the risk manager simply make recommendations without having the power to decide and act."

Carl wiped mustard from the corner of his mouth, dropped the napkin in a basket, and sat on a bench in the shade. Igor was startled by this reaction; he thought he had offended Carl and sat down in silence beside him.

"You're absolutely right," Carl said at last. "And you have no one to blame but yourself."

"Me?"

"Yes. You urged me to talk with Victoria Perez."

"Victoria told you to train your own risk manager?"

"No. She said risk management efforts could not be successful if they failed to mesh with an organization's culture. Well, we have a policy here, and it's a good one, I think, to hire from within. It makes sense. We have a lot of sharp people with few opportunities for advancement. Should I start off on the wrong foot by seeking an exception to that policy? Then, a risk management professional would be frustrated. Too little autonomy, too little ability to make decisions alone and act on them. That's not our style. My phone would be ringing off the hook, with everyone in an uproar about the risk management police snooping around and telling people what to do. The way I see it is we need someone familiar with our operation who will have the patience to persuade us and educate us and nudge us along gradually."

"Enough," Igor said. "You're right. I'm wrong. I had another model in mind—a corporate model. But what you're recommending will clearly work best for Urban."

The Hiring Decision

Carl used his statement of objectives, list of activities, and draft of a job description for the Risk Manager to explain his plans to Paula Unruh. She once again realized that he had developed his recommendation carefully. She authorized him to fill the position.

The job description was circulated throughout the university. Personnel selected three of seven applicants to meet with Carl. He interviewed them and eventually offered the job to Rita McGoff of the Legal Affairs department, who accepted the offer.

SUMMARY

Risk managers try to minimize the three types of costs of risk by pursuing objectives that support the organization's goals and reflect the organization's culture. Some of the skills needed to do that involve information gathering and analysis and the ability to motivate, persuade, and work with others. The emphasis on technical or managerial skills can reflect the nature and mission of the organization. An industrial risk engaged in hazardous activities is likely to emphasize loss prevention and reduction. A nonprofit organization not subject to specialized hazards is likely to emphasize coordination and advocacy skills. In either case, the support of the senior management of the organization is crucial for the success of the risk management program.

Just as all risk managers, regardless of the kind of organization they work for, are primarily engaged in performing the five steps in the risk management process, all risk managers perform those steps in order to reduce the three types of costs of risk while striving to achieve pre-loss and post-loss objectives. These types of cost of risk are (1) the lives, property, income, or other things of value damaged or destroyed in accidents; (2) the loss of potential profits or benefits that could have been gained through the ownership of assets or participation in activities that were avoided as too risky; and (3) the resources devoted to managing accidental losses that could have been otherwise employed. The benefits of risk management are reductions in the first two types of cost of risk—actual losses and lost opportunities. The third type of cost of risk is the cost of risk management. Risk management programs are designed to minimize all three types of cost of risk while helping the organization achieve its objectives.

Pre-loss risk management objectives have value whether a loss occurs or not. Economy of operation, tolerable uncertainty, and meeting legal requirements are typical pre-loss risk management objectives. Post-loss risk management objectives include the minimal condition an organization's senior management can accept following the most severe foreseeable loss. Survival and stability of earnings represent potential post-loss risk management objectives.

REVIEW QUESTIONS AND EXERCISES

1. Define or describe each of the words and phrases listed below:

    (a) Costs of risk

    (b) Pre-loss objectives

    (c) Post-loss objectives

    (d) Cost of risk management

    (e) Benefits of risk management

2. Organizational culture is a vague term. Based on the way it is used in the chapter, briefly explain it and give an example of it.

3. Exhibit 4-5 contains a draft of a job description for a risk manager. Revise and improve it based on what you have learned so far in this course.

4. Based on your revision of the job description, list three attributes of a successful risk manager.

5. Why does Bryan International Group devote a full-time position to property loss prevention?

6. Give two advantages of aligning risk management objectives with organizational objectives.

7. Write a brief explanation of the benefits of risk management in your own words.

8. Carl thought that the risk management function at Urban should be seen as "interdepartmental." Why?

9. Briefly evaluate Carl's reasons for recommending that Urban's new risk manager be assigned to the Treasurer's office.

ANSWERS TO ASSIGNMENT 4 QUESTIONS

1. (Define key terms)

2. Organizational culture is the set of values, beliefs, and norms that unites members of an organization. An organization could value the bottom line above all or could value quality customer service above all. A risk management program should be attuned to an organization's culture and should be aligned with the organization's goals.

3. Add the following to Duties in the job description:

    *   Examining the feasibility of alternative risk management techniques

    *   Selecting the most appropriate risk management techniques

    *   Implementing the chosen risk management techniques

    *   Monitoring and improving the risk management program

    *   Communicating the goals and importance of the risk management program

    Add the following to Requirements:

    *   Hold the CPCU and ARM designations

4. Three attributes of a successful risk manager are (1) knowledge of all the steps in the risk management process; (2) ability to communicate clearly, both in writing and in speaking; and (3) patience to gradually persuade and educate the organization.

5. Bryan International Group handles hazardous materials and manages highly protected risks. Bryan moved to a more aggressive program for managing risks. Also, the company encountered difficulty in obtaining product liability insurance, so it formed a captive insurance company to write this coverage. These challenges and changes warranted a full time risk manager.

6. Two advantages of aligning risk management objectives with organizational objectives are as follows:

    *   When risk management objectives are aligned with the organization's objectives, the risk manager is able to illustrate how the risk management process will further the organization's goals.

    *   The risk manager will gain credibility and help employees see the value of risk management.

7. In general, the benefits of risk management include reducing actual losses and lost opportunities and minimizing the cost of risk for an organization. Specific benefits include providing peace of mind to the stakeholders in the organization by managing risk, keeping the organization safer for its employees and customers, allowing the business to remain in operation after losses, and saving the organization money by lowering its insurance premium.

8. To most effectively identify and analyze the organization's risks and to best measure and evaluate the results of the risk management program, Urban's risk management functions should be interdepartmental. Carl believed that the feedback from the university's senior management and department heads was essential to accomplish this and to evaluate the performance of the risk manager.

9. Carl believed that the risk manager should report to him because insurance is an important part of the risk management program and financial records will be important for exposure identification and analysis. Carl also believed that he was most familiar with the goals he wants to accomplish at the university.

Assignment 5

BEFORE YOU BEGIN

Assignment 5 is the culmination of what you've learned in Assignments 1 through 4. It looks at risk management in action in a large, complex organization that is suddenly faced with a bewildering array of losses and potential losses. What you should gain from this assignment is the sense that the concepts you have learned in this course—the types of loss exposures, the steps in the risk management process, the methods and tools available for identifying and analyzing loss exposures, the risk control and risk financing techniques available for treating loss exposures, and the managerial and technical aspects of the risk management function—are sufficient to allow you to understand and explain to others how risk management works in even a relatively complex setting.

EDUCATIONAL OBJECTIVES FOR ASSIGNMENT 5

After completing this assignment, you should be able to:

1. Describe the relationship between an organization's risk management program and that organization's mission and objectives.

2. Explain to others the role of an organization's risk manager.

3. Describe the relationship between disaster planning and risk management.

4. Given a description of risk management in action at a given organization, be able to identify:

    (a) the four types of loss exposures;

(b) the five steps in the risk management process;

(c) the tools and methods for analyzing loss exposures;

(d) risk control techniques;

(e) risk financing techniques; and

(f) the technical (line) and managerial (staff) functions performed by the risk manager.

OUTLINE OF REQUIRED READING

  I. Background on Urban University
 II. The Event
III. The Risk Management Challenge
    A. Pre-loss objectives
        1. Economy of operations
        2. Tolerable uncertainty
        3. Legality
        4. Humanitarian conduct
    B. Post-loss objectives
        1. Survival
        2. Continuity of operations
        3. Profitability
        4. Stability of earnings
        5. Growth
        6. Humanitarian Conduct
    C. The risk management program
    D. Risk management objectives
    E. Risk management and the insurance response
 IV. Summary

Chapter **5**
Risk Management in Action

Becoming Urban University's new risk manager did not automatically turn Rita McGoff into a morning person. But she was ambitious and enthusiastic about her new job, and she realized she had much to learn. She soon trained herself to arrive at the office early, in order to ease the transition as she took up her new duties.

She met with Carl Francis and gained a clearer idea of the objectives he hoped the risk management program at Urban would achieve. She also met with Igor Buchenzenko, who provided her with a summary of Urban's insurance program and its coverages, conditions, and costs. Rita also realized that despite her years of employment at the university, she needed to learn more about it and to start to look at it in a new way.

BACKGROUND ON URBAN UNIVERSITY

Urban University's main campus, located in a large city neighborhood, has dormitories and housing for 6,000 undergraduate and graduate students in addition to classrooms, research laboratories, and administrative offices in numerous buildings. In addition, the campus includes sports facilities, galleries, libraries, theaters, book and sundry goods stores, and other similar service and recreational facilities available to the students and to the residents of neighboring communities. Urban also supports a student radio and television facility and links all dorm residents, classes, and employees to a computer network system that is also linked to the Internet.

Urban staffs a student infirmary with professionals affiliated with the city hospital bordering the campus. The university also employs armed, uniformed security officers who patrol the campus buildings and grounds. Its fleet of maintenance and transport vehicles is garaged on campus. Urban even operates an incineration facility on campus for its waste materials.

The university also maintains a suburban campus for educational programs to which students commute, and some students live nearby in privately owned or rented housing. The campus is composed of classroom and administrative buildings and some athletic facilities, including a stadium for Urban's varsity sports programs.

Urban's president reports to a board of trustees who are responsible for governing the university. Urban's charter establishes the university as a nonprofit institution and states that its mission is to provide superior higher education and to serve as a research pioneer and a community service leader.

With the trustees' approval, the president appoints directors to manage academic programs, admissions, financial development, student activities, university administration, and community affairs. The university's treasurer and legal affairs director also reports directly to the president.

THE EVENT

Rita's learning curve took an unexpected upswing as the result of one element of her job description that had been little more than an afterthought to Carl Francis: "serves on the committee responsible for the University's Emergency Operations Plan." Carl had not found the time to take an active part in this committee. He thought assigning the responsibility to Rita would provide her with an opportunity to learn more about the other departments of the university. He also realized that risk management and disaster planning are related, and he thought participation on the committee would help Rita develop a risk management program for the university.

Soon after she became the university's new risk manager, Rita received a call from Urban's safety director to discuss a final draft of the Emergency Operations Plan. The plan depended on an emergency operations center (EOC) where representatives of the university's administration would gather to coordinate emergency response and restore the university's operating conditions after a major storm or another disaster. Only eighteen months earlier, a tornado had struck Urban along with other parts of the city, resulting in heavy damage to buildings and a shutdown of communications that caused Urban to cancel classes and other planned events for a week. Rita saw a clear connection between the Emergency Operations Plan and the post-loss risk management objective of survival that Carl Francis had described to her.

Two days after Rita spoke with the safety director, the jury in a racially charged trial handed down an unexpectedly controversial decision, and

Urban's city, like some others across the country, erupted in rioting, looting, fires, and power outages, including the area immediately adjacent to Urban's main campus.

Beginning the afternoon of the verdict, a Monday during Urban's spring term, reports of off-campus violence, fires, and looting began to flood Urban's security office. The security director initiated the first stage of the Emergency Operations Plan: deploying the security officers into a prearranged schedule of duty, two twelve-hour shifts in which all officers were either on duty or on standby. In addition, he ordered all campus entrances closed except one that security officers would monitor.

Early that evening, an Urban student was attacked outside the front entrance of the campus, and Urban's emergency medical technicians (EMTs) responded by treating the student and transporting him to the city hospital for additional treatment. Later that evening, Urban's security officers encountered a nonuniversity person who had been shot at a street corner, issued orders for people to clear the area, and directed EMTs to treat the victim. After waiting forty minutes for a city ambulance, security officers provided escort for a city fire department rescue ambulance unable to leave its nearby station without such protection. Later, Urban's infirmary physician and nurse, who had volunteered to come in from their homes, treated numerous victims of assaults just off campus. Since no ambulances were by then available, officers improvised, taking the seats out of a university van to convert it into a temporary ambulance.

Major fires raged off campus and a few fires erupted on campus, including one in a residence building basement trash receptacle, which triggered the sprinkler protection system, flooding the ground floor rooms and offices. In addition, two students sustained gunshot wounds while watching events from exposed dormitory balconies. Maintenance workers, also on overtime duty, emptied and secured all large trash receptacles and Dumpsters. Residence advisors moved students affected by the dorm fire to other rooms, and the wounded students received EMT treatment and transport to the hospital.

Conditions surrounding the campus continued to deteriorate by Tuesday morning, so the president activated the EOC. Most faculty and administrative personnel who had left campus on Monday did not return on Tuesday morning. Yet 5,000 students remained in the dorms and university housing on campus and within the neighborhood immediately off campus. As the result of the president's order, the security, maintenance, facilities, residences, dining, transportation, and telecommunications directors now reported to the EOC.

In light of the continued looting of nearby businesses and the slow or lack of response of city fire and police personnel, the president and EOC suspended activities at the main campus but directed activities to continue at the suburban campus, which was relatively unaffected by the civil unrest. Public relations disseminated to the media an announcement informing students that classes and examinations would be postponed until the following week.

Telecommunications established bulletins on the campus network. Calls from students and parents to the hotline EOC had opened were referred to student affairs staff for response. During four hours on Tuesday morning, a power outage intermittently interrupted the hotline and network communications. The student TV station continued to transmit by generator, agreeing to broadcast Urban's periodic official bulletins.

After renewed attacks by gangs against students off campus, EOC directed transportation and security services to bring to the campus all students in university-owned residential properties off campus and to locate them in temporary shelters in recreation facilities. Dining Services established a twenty-four-hour food service for residents, EOC staff, and, as it turned out, city emergency workers, including police and fire personnel trapped in the area. Since suppliers had refused to make deliveries to the campus, security details were dispatched to escort service suppliers with linens and food on campus.

Organized patrols of EOC staff with flashlights, fire extinguishers, and two-way radios served as building-watch teams to report intruders or vandalism around campus buildings. Among the incidents the teams encountered and tried to mediate were disputes between students and staff regarding the motives for the unrest. Some of the disputes led to fighting and property damage, including to the cameras and microphones of student reporters trying to capture the controversy for their programs.

By Wednesday, Paula Unruh, Urban's president, determined that the campus should begin to return to normal operations as soon as reasonably feasible, including reopening the campus gates, library, and bookstore, and reinstituting the Open Door Policy for use of the gym by neighborhood children. The university respected the city's dawn-to-dusk curfew by maintaining building-watch teams. Public relations and telecommunications services conveyed revised examination, class, and community event schedules through the media and the computer network.

THE RISK MANAGEMENT CHALLENGE

Rita immediately faced a multitude of risk management issues arising out of these events, issues that were not limited to the incidents of bodily injury and property damage on campus or against university community members. She began her evaluation of the event by revisiting Urban's mission statement: superior educator; research pioneer; and community leader. Had the Emergency Operations Plan been developed and implemented in support of this mission? Had implementation created more risks than it had averted? Was the plan consistent with the university's risk management objectives? This last question reminded Rita that she had yet to develop a written risk management program, her first priority on taking the new job.

She decided to use the event and the Emergency Operations Plan as the platform for developing her risk management program. She recognized that the event provided her the opportunity to show senior management the importance of an effective program with clear pre-loss and post-loss objectives.

Pre-Loss Objectives

Rita began by reconsidering pre-loss objectives in the light of what she had learned from the recent emergency.

Economy of Operations

Rita knew that Urban's shrinking budget had caused the university to discontinue certain academic programs and cut back on other administrative resources. She wondered whether the emergency operations planners had developed a budget for the plan or had otherwise identified the sources of funds that implementing the plan would require. Even though the plan was designed to respond to emergencies, Rita believed that economy should still be factored into operational decisions. She also wondered whether the planners had considered which costs could be covered by existing or available insurance or other risk transfer methods, such as indemnification from the city for costs the university had incurred while performing duties citizens expect the city to execute.

Tolerable Uncertainty

Certainly, the plan served as a framework for response to emergencies that should reduce managers' uncertainty regarding their roles in controlling the damage from a disaster. The plan's features—including centralized decision making, comprehensive communications, and the organized physical presence of university officials—should also calm the university and surrounding communities, as well as parents and benefactors.

Rita decided to assess whether these intended results were achieved in light of technological breakdowns and isolation from surrounding city emergency systems. Did the plan provide for adequate backup procedures when key personnel, technology, and city links were unavailable or inoperative?

Legality

The legality objective was Rita's greatest concern. Did the plan tacitly encourage university personnel to operate outside the local, state, or federal laws or to act in a potentially negligent fashion that exposed Urban to civil liability? She worried about the effects of activities during each day of the emergency, particularly those of the security officers and medical personnel.

She was concerned about the limits of their authority and professional responsibility off campus and toward people who were not university community members. What were Urban's responsibilities with regard to notification of public authorities when exercising policing and emergency medical treatment and the transport of nonuniversity people off campus?

Rita questioned whether Urban's workers compensation insurance policy would cover injuries sustained by university members who volunteered their time or otherwise functioned outside the normal scope of their duties. And could the university enjoy immunities from liability created for governmental agencies that perform health and safety services, even if the university had not extended its resources to the general public surrounding the campus?

Had the university members who formed patrols exceeded their authority in intervening in violent disputes? Would the university share responsibility or carry full responsibility for damage to the student press equipment? And what about the veracity and propriety of the student broadcasts, which carried beyond the campus? Rita suspected that, having enlisted the station's cooperation early in the emergency to communicate official bulletins, Urban might have some liability for its other broadcast activities.

Humanitarian Conduct

Rita was certain that the plan's existence evidenced Urban's commitment to good citizenship and social responsibility. She did wonder whether the "good Samaritan" concept would shield licensed professionals from liability if the plan directed service beyond Urban's borders by university security officers, EMTs, and health-care professionals who responded to EOC direction during the emergency.

Post-Loss Objectives

In a similar way, Rita reconsidered post-loss objectives.

Survival

Rita recognized the importance of the plan for Urban's survival in the event of a disaster. She intended to closely evaluate whether the plan's design addressed each of the four major categories of loss, any of which, alone or in combination, could permanently close Urban's doors:

- Property

- Net income (or, in Urban's case, revenues and endowment)

- Liability

- Personnel

She considered the first two categories as inevitably tied to Urban's overall survival planning. Rita knew she had to learn more about the development office's contingency plans and those of the other revenue-producing facilities, such as the bookstore or the theater, as well as evaluate the business interruption and extra expense insurance coverage Urban had in place. For example, she quickly learned that such insurance would not cover the expenses Urban incurred to feed, house, and provide transport for or medical treatment to nonuniversity personnel. She also needed to determine how much physical damage or revenue losses resulting from civil unrest Urban's insurance would reimburse. Finally, Rita recognized that the emergency operations plan did not address the noninsurance risk financing techniques, including the investment practices needed to protect Urban's revenues.

She thought it unlikely that actions Urban's personnel took during a genuine emergency could subject the university to a crippling legal judgment. Instead, she intended to focus on actions the university might take beyond its charter or legal authority that could render Urban vulnerable to governmentally imposed suspension of key activities, such as research or fund-raising development. Threats to Urban's nonprofit status could impose devastating tax burdens on the institution.

Rita knew that Urban was rich in talented personnel who could readily replace key operational and senior management in most circumstances. She was more concerned about the potential loss of distinguished faculty and researchers who attracted funding and renown to Urban, in turn attracting exceptional students and other prominent scholars. Urban's survival might depend on protection of these individuals or the resources they expected to have accessible.

Continuity of Operations

Rita recognized that one goal of the emergency plan functions is to minimize disruption of Urban's normal operations as long as possible. The president, in this case, had not canceled classes and other activities until twenty-four hours after activating the plan's initial stage. Even then, the president directed that operations at Urban's suburban campus continue. Rita decided to determine whether more main campus operations could be transferred to the suburban campus, a risk control technique that could minimize disruption of the institution's core functions (holding classes, giving examinations, conducting research, and so on).

Here again, Rita recognized that financing the extra expense of continuing operations in the face of limited emergencies would be important, as would restoring revenues lost during an emergency, including tuition, grants, and development funds, that had been budgeted for long-term continuation of operations.

Profitability

Rita learned from Carl Francis that Urban treads a fine line between its privilege to amass resources in support of its mission, comprising an endowment, and its responsibility to governmental agencies, such as the IRS and grant-funding agencies, to avoid profit-making in order to retain its non-taxable status and eligibility for public funds. She thought that stability of earnings, rather than profitability, might provide the university with a more ambitious post-loss objective than survival without jeopardizing the institution's nonprofit status.

Stability of Earnings

Urban is probably permitted to engage in risk financing activities that set aside funds outside an endowment without jeopardizing its charter and non-profit status in order to stabilize its budget during periods of severe or frequent losses. For example, Urban could divert revenues to fund a self-insurance account or a trust in anticipation of projected losses from catastrophes, such as the recent event, for which insurance will not compensate its losses. Moreover, other governmental agencies, such as the Environmental Protection Agency (EPA), may require Urban to evidence sufficient financial security to address environmental hazards arising from its operations, such as the operation of its incineration plant or the need to dispose of hazardous materials researchers store and use in its laboratories. Crises such as the recent event or the earlier tornado could easily trigger losses associated with environmental hazards.

Growth

Urban's "Plan for the Future" includes ambitious new academic program objectives, including new inter-professional school degrees and virtual class-room remote education programs. Although these plans may not increase Urban's physical size or staff, its development into new areas of operation challenge Rita to reexamine the Emergency Operations Plan's success in preserving Urban's timetable for such expansion. Serious physical damage and substantial diversion of revenues to recover from this crisis could force Urban to forgo an expansion opportunity or lose its funding for such pioneering programs to another institution.

Humanitarian Conduct

Rita wondered whether the aggressiveness with which the EOC addressed this objective may have compromised Urban's ability to achieve some other post-loss objectives. At a minimum, she will determine whether Urban can secure advance commitments from governmental authorities that they will offset or reimburse Urban's cost to contribute to public health and safety during periods of reduced public services. Otherwise, Urban may need to weigh its role as good citizen against its fiscal constraints and the demands of other pre-loss and post-loss risk management objectives. She planned to ask senior management to revisit the potential conflict among the three elements of Urban's mission—education, research, and public service—and set priorities for them to provide guidance for the university's risk management objectives.

The Risk Management Program

Rita's participation in the EOC and her experience with the plan in action have given her a basis for clarifying the university's risk management objectives, an opportunity to establish her position within the university administration, a chance to detail the resources she requires and the authority she must exercise to achieve the objectives, and the ability to document her plan appropriately as part of Urban's central policies and procedures. She will seek Carl Francis's approval of the plan and the public support of the president for it. Rita also realizes that the rapport she developed with the representatives of key units during the EOC's operation will help her gain their cooperation when implementing an effective, coordinated risk management program.

By evaluating the emergency operation plan's performance, Rita in effect performed step five of the risk management process—monitoring and improving the risk management program. As a result, she also set in motion the first two steps in the process—exposure identification and analysis and examining alternative treatment techniques. So long as she considers possibilities beyond the single event and contingencies if circumstances had occurred differently, she will have the opportunity to plan from reality rather than designing a program in a vacuum. Her collaboration with other institutional constituencies in designing and implementing the plan will not only increase support for it but also result in further refinement to include values, perils, and financial consequences for the university that others can better anticipate than she.

Risk Management Objectives

Rita's understanding of the university's risk management objectives, based on her talks with Carl Francis, might be stated this way:

- Preserve the institution's assets

- Minimize disruption of operations

- Reduce overall cost of risk

Rita's principal concern throughout the recent emergency was whether the EOC's centralized decision-making process might have duplicated or blurred the distinct responsibilities of different Urban departments. Recognizing that her position is new, she still wonders what specific responsibilities of hers may have been overlooked before and during the committee-directed activities of those three intense days when the plan was in operation.

As the result of these concerns and considerations, Rita resolved to articulate risk management objectives and procedures that neither imitate those of another department nor exceed her position's authority. Accordingly, she considered that the above objectives describe too generally those shared by other administrative areas, like the treasurer's office or the security department.

Rita decided that the distinguishing characteristic for a risk management position, no matter what its reporting lines or resources may be, is a continuous reapplication of the risk management process. Exhibit 5-1 details the activities that make up the steps in that process.

Exhibit 5-1
Steps in the Risk Management Decision-Making Process

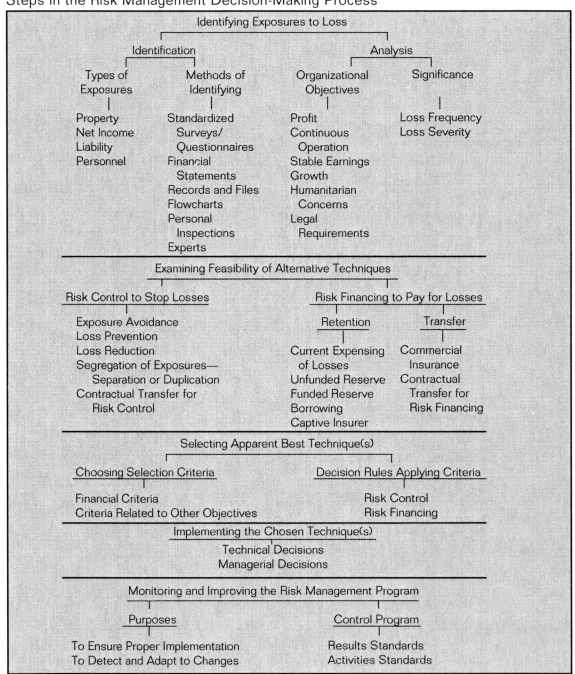

The common thread among most risk management programs she had reviewed were such activities as "assisting," "reviewing," "developing," "negotiating," "advising," "reporting," and "approving." She determined to become the university's expert at executing the risk management process, even though she would need to rely on Urban's legal, financial, analytical, and safety experts, as well as its management and insurance consultants, for the specialized knowledge necessary to conduct the process.

Risk Management and the Insurance Response

Rita intends to take a number of actions related to future implementation of the Emergency Operations Plan.

First, she will urge the university's legal and security representatives to review the plan with local and regional officials. At the same time, she will become familiar with the governmental emergency procedures to determine the level of cooperation expected of the university by those authorities. Her aim is to prearrange effective lines of communication should another emergency engulf the university and the surrounding city to ensure the efficient, authorized deployment of all available resources. She expects that the goodwill Urban's assistance built with authorities during the recent crisis will improve the likelihood of planned sharing of resources in the future.

Second, Rita will work with her insurance broker to review the plan with Urban's liability insurance carriers so that the underwriting and claims representatives understand the plan's goals and the structure of the EOC's authority. In this way, she might avoid the possibility that the carriers would decline to cover claims that might arise during the plan's activation from decisions made by individuals or under circumstances outside the typical university framework. Among other potential claims that concern her are those against Urban for bodily injury or property damage by the nonuniversity people whom Urban emergency personnel treated or restrained, or for nuisance or business losses asserted by neighbors resulting from Urban's involvement in the safety or security of their neighborhood. Similarly, the carrier providing professional liability coverage to the emergency and licensed medical professionals would be prepared for claims arising from their activities beyond the scope of their usual duties for Urban. This preapproval process addresses several risk management objectives, including pre-loss reduction of uncertainty and post-loss stability of earnings.

Rita confirmed with Urban's automobile liability carrier that, if authorized by governmental authorities, the carrier will extend liability and physical damage coverage if claims arise when the university's vehicles are converted from their intended uses to emergency transport or evacuation shuttles. Further, she extended coverage to the liability of employees who operate their own personal vehicles during an emergency. Under these circumstances, employees no longer depend on their own insurance coverage in the event of a claim or loss. Each of these measures will address the post-loss objectives of continuity of operations and stability of earnings over the long run.

Rita now appreciates more fully the importance of anticipating the range of events that can disrupt Urban's ability to fulfill its mission as part of her exposure identification and analysis responsibilities. She intends to review with Igor the exclusions and limits of the university's insurance coverage, especially with regard to (1) property damages arising from a riot or public disturbance and (2) lost business revenue and extra expenses incurred to resume operations.

Rita realized that even though the plan's design and the EOC's dedication possibly reduced loss of life and probably accelerated Urban's return to business, Urban's property insurance coverages will probably not reimburse significant financial losses. Rita urged Igor Buchenzenko to determine the circumstances under which certain terms of the insurance may be renegotiated. She also approached Carl Francis, the treasurer, to discuss risk financing measures in addition to insurance, such as a funded reserve or a particular investment program that might help Urban meet such contingent losses in the future, regardless of the cause of loss.

In the course of reviewing Urban's property insurance policy's responsiveness to recent events, Rita identified exposures she needs to reevaluate. For example, she learned that Urban houses its accounts receivables operations in a leased suite of offices in a building just off campus that narrowly avoided fire damage during the crisis. The receipts valuation for insurance purposes was done ten years ago, and the sublimits provided in the property policy for loss of receipts are substantially inadequate.

In addition, from a risk management standpoint, Rita is concerned that Urban's lease with the building owner does not provide release from continued rental payments if circumstances like those arising from the recent crisis prevent Urban staff from gaining access to the premises. She will ask her old boss in the Legal Affairs Department to review and, if possible, renegotiate the terms of the lease.

Rita has confirmed that Urban's general liability policy will cover claims of defamation against Urban arising out of the student broadcasts. Still, she prefers to encourage compliance with existing guidelines under which students can use university communications apparatus. She would rather avoid losses than seek additional insurance coverage for the student journalists likely to be included in the same claim. She intends to work with the student activities administrators to reinforce the risk management responsibilities of student advisors and managers. She can take advantage of this contact to encourage the participation of the leaders of student activities in future discussions of the Emergency Operations Plan so that they can contribute to its effective implementation if emergency circumstances arise again. Once these decisions have been acted on, Rita can monitor the success of the plan itself.

SUMMARY

Urban University's Emergency Operations Plan is not a risk management program. It is a series of loss prevention and loss reduction steps to be taken at the president's discretion under extraordinary circumstances. These steps range from the deployment of increased numbers of security officers, through limiting access to the university, to the temporary cessation of classes and other activities in conjunction with a centralization of administrative decision making.

The plan should become an integral part of a coordinated risk management program. Nonetheless, implementation of the plan gave Rita a basis for preparing a risk management plan for the university.

First, because of Rita's new responsibilities, she can bring a risk management perspective to the plan itself and to an evaluation of how it worked in action. This perspective shows itself in Rita's consideration of the plan in terms of, first, the university's mission and, second, the university's possible pre-loss and post-loss risk management objectives. Rita is aware that she lacks the authority to determine these objectives herself, but she can have the university's senior managers reconsider them, resolve potential conflicts between objectives, and establish priorities for the objectives.

Second, Rita's knowledge of the four types of loss exposures gives her a framework that brings order to an otherwise chaotic array of losses. Applying this framework to the losses and potential losses that arose during the implementation of the emergency operation plan allows Rita to begin identifying and analyzing the university's loss exposures.

Third, Rita's familiarity with the steps in the risk management process permits her to look at the events from a financial as well as from a safety standpoint. She could determine the extent to which insurance coverages would finance the losses the university suffered and to begin to consider additional insurance coverages and the use of other risk financing techniques in the future. She can also introduce some additional risk control techniques—involving students in the emergency operations planning process to avoid losses, for example. Fourth, Rita's recognition that risk management is a continuous application of a process enables her to propose short-term improvements to the university's Emergency Operations Plan while realizing that it will need to be monitored and improved in the future.

Finally, Rita has become rapidly aware of the managerial and technical aspects of the risk manager's role. She has determined to become the university's expert in applying the risk management process but understands that will require her to work with others, drawing on their expertise.

Rita's experience has shown that she has much to learn, but also that her understanding of some basic risk management terms and tools has already enabled her to improve the university's ability to manage risk.

REVIEW QUESTIONS AND EXERCISES

1. Classify each of the following exposures by type (property, liability, personnel, or net income):

    (a) Flooding of a dormitory by a sprinkler released by fire.

    (b) Transporting sufferers of injuries to a nearby hospital.

    (c) Cessation of classes and other operations.

    (d) Treatment of nonuniversity community members by university medical staff.

2. Classify each of the following techniques for treating losses as either a *risk control* technique or a *risk financing* technique.

    (a) Establishing an alternative place to hold classes at a suburban campus to minimize disruption of operations.

    (b) Renegotiating a lease on an office to avoid payment of rent when access to the property is denied.

    (c) The deductibles in a property insurance policy.

    (d) Earmarking an investment fund to offset projected uninsured losses.

(e) Training sessions for emergency medical treatment personnel.

(f)   Negotiating reimbursement from city officials for services provided during an emergency.

(g) Cancellation of classes and other activities on campus.

(h) Increasing hours of duty for security guards.

(i)   Establishing a hotline to provide parents with information.

(j)   A sprinkler system in a dormitory.

3. Briefly explain why Rita's experience with Urban's Emergency Operations Plan can be considered performing the fifth step in the risk management process.

4. Rita decided to recommend a change in Urban's risk management objectives. Was she acting in a *line* or *staff* capacity when making that recommendation? Explain the reasons for your answer.

5. Rita thought Urban should look into obtaining backup communications equipment for use in case of an emergency. Identify and describe the risk control technique this recommendation represents.

6. A decline in Urban's reputation could decrease its ability to raise funds. Does the chance of reduced fund raising represent a pure or a speculative risk? Give reasons for your answer.

7. When Rita meets with Igor Buchenzenko to review insurance policy provisions, which method of analyzing loss exposures is she using? Give reasons for your answers.

8. Describe how Rita might determine the financial consequences for Urban involved in the destruction of a university dormitory by fire.

9. Briefly describe the relationship between disaster planning and risk management.

ANSWERS TO ASSIGNMENT 5 QUESTIONS

1. Exposure classifications:

    a. Flooding of a dormitory by a sprinkler released by fire—property

    b. Transporting the injured to a nearby hospital—liability

    c. Cessation of classes and other operations—net income

    d. Treatment of non-university community members by university medical staff—liability

2. Classification of techniques for treating losses:

    a. Establishing an alternative place to hold classes—risk control: duplication

    b. Renegotiating office lease—risk financing: transfer

    c. Property insurance deductibles—risk financing: retention

    d. Earmarking an investment fund to offset projected uninsured losses—risk financing: retention

    e. Holding training sessions for emergency medical treatment personnel—risk control: loss reduction

    f. Negotiating reimbursement from city officials for services provided during an emergency—risk financing: contractual transfer

    g. Cancellation of classes and other activities on campus—risk control: avoidance

    h. Increasing hours of duty for security guards—risk control: loss prevention

    i. Establishing a hotline to provide parents with information—risk control: loss reduction

    j. Installing a sprinkler system in a dormitory—risk control: loss reduction

3. The fifth step in the risk management process is monitoring and improving the risk management program. Rita's Emergency Operations Plan would accomplish this step because, after a disaster, Rita can identify alternative treatment techniques for exposures identified.

4. Rita was acting in a staff capacity. Rita lacks the authority to determine risk management objectives. However, she can have the university's senior managers reconsider the objectives, resolve potential conflicts among objectives, and establish priorities for the objectives.

5. Rita was recommending the risk control technique of duplication, which is a way of segregating exposures.

6. Reduced fund raising would be a pure risk because it could result in a loss or no loss. Unlike a speculative risk, it could not result in a gain.

7. When Rita meets with Igor Buchenzenko to review insurance policy provisions, she is consulting with an expert to analyze loss exposures. Igor is an insurance broker with his CPCU and ARM designations.

8. To determine the financial consequences for Urban of the dormitory's destruction, Rita can analyze the University's financial statements. These statements would indicate the value of the dormitory and its contents as well as the income generated by the dormitory.

9. A disaster plan is a series of loss prevention and loss reduction steps to be taken under extraordinary circumstances. The disaster plan is an integral part of the risk management plan.

Assignment 6

BEFORE YOU BEGIN

The first five assignments have prepared you to achieve the primary objectives of this course—to help you understand what risk managers do, how they do it, and why it is important.

To accomplish that, we have considered some scenarios that are slightly unrealistic or at least out of the ordinary. Rita McGoff's drive to work is a simpler risk management problem than the problems that risk managers generally handle. Rita's being confronted early in her career with multiple losses and exposures and disaster planning, on the other hand, is a more complex situation than most risk managers meet.

This assignment has two objectives: first, to provide an opportunity for you to review some of the material covered earlier, and second, to show how the risk management process might work in several brief, realistic settings. In short, this assignment should help assure that you understand how risk management works in the real world.

EDUCATIONAL OBJECTIVES FOR ASSIGNMENT 6

After completing this assignment, you should be able to perform all of the objectives for Assignments 1-5 *and* have a better idea of how risk management actually works in the business world. (You should also then be ready to take and pass the examination for this course.) Remember as you read these scenarios that you are not responsible for knowledge of the details of the problems presented but only for understanding how risk management problems can emerge, be analyzed, and be solved through an application of the five steps in the risk management process.

OUTLINE OF REQUIRED READING

Chapter 6

Risk Management at Work

Risk management is a technique that is growing in importance because it helps organizations to achieve their goals and objectives, financial and otherwise. The following brief case studies show how risk management helps to accomplish that on a day-to-day basis.

THE PERSONNEL EXPOSURE AND THE FATE OF FAILSAFE

Failsafe was originally a partnership organized by two friends who recognized a need for a central monitoring station that could monitor and respond to the alarm systems of a wide variety of clients. The two friends, Charles Deal and Al Smyth, had many years of experience in law enforcement and firefighting, respectively. They concluded that between them they had the necessary expertise to service a range of clients with various types of alarm systems and to recruit and train an appropriate staff if the number of clients grew.

Time proved them to be correct, and Failsafe gradually became very successful. The aptitudes and temperaments of the two partners contributed greatly to the success of the firm. Charles Deal was primarily responsible for marketing Failsafe's services—keeping in touch with clients and finding new ones. Al Smyth, on the other hand, ran Failsafe's operations, developed its response procedures, hired and trained employees, and managed the office and staff. In time, Failsafe incorporated. Charles Deal became president and chief executive officer of the corporation and owned 45 percent of the corporation's stock. Al Smyth became the executive vice president and chief operating officer of Failsafe, Inc., and also owned 45 percent of the corporation's stock.

Despite Failsafe's role as a provider of safety and security—in effect, risk control—services, the owners never took a systematic approach to the risk management of their own organization. As a result, the magnitude of the personnel exposure faced by the corporation because of the expertise, contacts, and ownership represented by Charles Deal and Al Smyth, Failsafe's two key employees, went unrecognized and virtually untreated. In March of last year, Deal and Smyth both died in an airplane crash while they were on a rare business trip together. This tragic loss drove Failsafe out of business. Neither the remaining staff members employed by the corporation nor the surviving family members who inherited 90 percent of the corporation's stock felt capable of continuing the business.

Many organizations prohibit two or more key employees from flying on the same airplane or establish some other policy with regard to air travel in order to limit the personnel exposure. Such a policy is a risk control technique intended to reduce the severity of a loss through *separation*. Although Failsafe, Inc., could not prevent the airplane crash, it could have significantly reduced its loss potential by requiring its two key executives to travel on separate planes.

If the nature and significance of Failsafe's personnel exposure had been identified and analyzed, other potential risk control and risk financing techniques could have been used to treat the exposure. *Duplication*, another risk control technique, would have identified potential replacements for the key executives and encouraged the firm to engage in succession planning, determining the future owners and managers of the business. In addition, a disaster recovery plan would have established procedures that would have permitted the corporation to continue to meet its clients' needs and continue to function, at least temporarily, allowing the heirs of the deceased executives the opportunity to decide what to do with the corporation in the long run. Instead of that, the heirs were forced to sell their shares to a competitor at what might be considered a bargain price.

The personnel exposure could also have been treated through the purchase of life insurance, with Failsafe, Inc., as both the owner and beneficiary of the life insurance policies. This risk financing technique could have provided sufficient funds to allow Failsafe to continue its operations, providing wages, salaries, and benefits to employees, services to clients, increased assets and opportunities to the heirs of the firm's founders, and continued well-being for the communities affected by Failsafe's existence.

Although Failsafe, Inc., never grew to such an extent that it would have been practical for the firm to hire a full-time risk manager, the firm's insurance agent or broker, a risk management consultant, or Al Smyth as office manager in cooperation with an outside expert could have applied the risk management process to the organization. If that had been done, the corporation's crucial personnel exposure would have been identified, analyzed, and treated—benefiting the owners, their employees, customers, and families, and the community at large. Exhibit 6-1 summarizes the techniques for treating Failsafe's personnel exposure.

Exhibit 6-1
Techniques for Treating Failsafe's Personnel Exposure

Risk Control
- Separation—Key executives required to fly on separate aircraft
- Duplication—Potential replacements for key executives identified, succession planning encouraged
- Disaster recovery plan—Procedures established to continue operations in the event of a disaster

Risk Financing
- Life insurance—Failsafe as owner and beneficiary of policies on lives of key executives

MYSTERIOUS DISAPPEARANCES

Stella Evans is the risk manager of StateMed, a large, nonprofit hospital that performs research activities as well as providing inpatient and outpatient care.

The director of StateMed's animal research lab recently asked Stella to purchase insurance that would reimburse the lab for the full cost of certain regularly disappearing equipment: scales, calipers, and electronic data processing equipment.

The director of the animal research lab explained to Stella that he had been trying to budget for the equipment by estimating how many replacements would be needed in a specific budget period. Because of increasing costs, however, the treasurer warned the director that this year, if losses continued at the current rate, insufficient funds would be available for replacements. The director was requesting the purchase of insurance so that replacements could be purchased even if budgetable funds were exhausted.

Stella assured the director that she appreciated having these losses drawn to her attention and that she was eager to solve his problem. But she also explained that simply purchasing insurance as he requested was not necessarily the best way of treating the exposure. Instead, Stella suggested that she analyze the exposure in cooperation with the director of the animal research lab and others.

Stella analyzed the exposure by interviewing not only the lab's director but also StateMed's security staff. She reviewed the lab's purchasing and equipment procedures. She also reviewed the organization's security logs.

Stella's investigation revealed the following facts:

1. The lab director was not aware that StateMed already maintained a property insurance policy that would have covered replacement of some of the missing equipment or the cost of its repair resulting from certain causes of damage.

2. Missing equipment was rarely, if ever, reported as theft, even though the most frequently taken items were those commonly known to be used in alleged drug manufacturing and distribution or items with relatively high values when resold (the computer equipment). No investigation had been conducted to identify internal suspects, points of lab security breached, or opportunities to recover missing equipment.

3. The director routinely approved reimbursements to research employees following their report of lost or damaged equipment they personally owned and used in their research, even if the losses occurred in employees' personal vehicles or at their homes. No policies existed to limit StateMed's responsibility for equipment lost, damaged, or stolen under these circumstances.

4. The lab had no maintenance agreements with equipment suppliers that could provide coverage for replacement or repair following loss or damage to equipment under certain circumstances.

Stella further noted these limitations of relying on insurance coverage:

- StateMed's broker confirmed that insurance purchased by the organization to cover missing or damaged equipment would limit coverage to the researcher's own lost or damaged physical and intellectual property.

- "First-dollar" replacement cost insurance coverage for all missing laboratory equipment invites lax equipment management and requires a costly price for what might better be handled through employee training and asset control.

- Reimbursement alone, whether from an insurance policy or out of the department budget, fails to consider the effect that thefts, false loss reports, and careless equipment management have on research progress and employee morale.

Stella Evans told the director of the lab that the lab should take advantage of the university's property insurance program—with the lab bearing an allocated portion of StateMed's premium cost—but only in combination with these measures:

1. Covered losses must be subject to a deductible (in addition to the lab's premium charge). The retained amount is to be allocated among the researchers and employees responsible for equipment based on their loss experience, providing an incentive to better protect the equipment. The preparation of a schedule of equipment for the insurance carrier will also improve the lab's equipment documentation procedures.

2. Stella's office will not submit insurance claims on the lab's behalf without a completed loss report form and, when appropriate, a report to

StateMed's security staff for investigation. The insurance carrier will require the organization to cooperate with such investigations, particularly if they could lead to the recovery of lost equipment.

3. The lab must enforce StateMed's policy that employees use their personally owned property at their own risk and may receive an incremental reimbursement for expected wear and tear of that property but *not* for replacement or repairs following loss or damage. (The lab can apply for exceptions to this policy if StateMed chooses not to purchase special pieces of equipment. If such an exception is granted, the property insurance carrier will individually schedule that equipment on the policy for coverage subject to evidence that maintenance and security procedures have been strictly followed.)

4. Stella Evans, as risk manager, is to receive and evaluate all maintenance agreements with equipment suppliers that offer coverage for repair or replacement of equipment that is lost or damaged under certain circumstances.

The lab director accepted Stella's recommendations and arranged for Stella to hold training sessions with lab staff to make them familiar with the recommendations and to assist with their implementation. Stella's recommendations solved the lab director's immediate budgeting problem and eventually significantly reduced claims for lost and damaged equipment.

In this case, the evaluation of a loss exposure led to the selection of risk control and risk financing techniques for treating that exposure: transfer for risk control (with respect to employee's personal equipment), loss reduction (through the implementation of reporting procedures, the involvement of StateMed's security people, and the improved documentation of equipment), retention (the allocation of the deductible to employees based on loss experience), and insurance. Rather than simply solving the lab director's budgeting problem, Stella's recommendations bring the lab's procedures in line with StateMed's policies, draw the attention of other departments (Security, for instance) to problems in the lab, and can help solve problems with a management style that could have led to more serious problems and losses in the future. Exhibit 6-2 summarizes the techniques for treating the exposures arising from the missing equipment.

OUT OF SIGHT, OUT OF MIND?

Early Warning, a manufacturer of alarm systems (fire alarms, burglar alarms, and so on) purchases the components for its products from several suppliers. The company uses only one source for some components, however. For instance, Early Warning purchases all metal cases required for its alarms from Family Owned Machine Shop, a small company located in Windy Town, approximately ten miles from the Atlantic Ocean.

In order to fabricate the alarm cases in accordance with Early Warning's specifications, Family Owned has care, custody, and control of patterns

Exhibit 6-2
Techniques for Treating Exposures Arising From
StateMed's Mysterious Disappearances

Risk Control
- Transfer for risk control (with respect to employees' personal equipment)
- Loss reduction through:
  - reporting procedures
  - involvement of StateMed's Security department
  - improved documentation
  - employee training

Risk Financing
- Retention—the use of deductible
- Insurance
- Potential noninsurance transfer based on review of contracts with equipment suppliers

---

and dies. This personal property is valued at a replacement cost of $35,000, is owned by Early Warning, and has been stored and used in Family Owned's shop for more than ten years. From a financial accounting standpoint, the property has been fully depreciated for three years, so it has no book value.

On September 4, a hurricane moved up the Atlantic coast and veered inland near Windy Town, causing substantial damage to Family Owned's building and equipment. Among the property destroyed were the patterns and dies owned by Early Warning. (They were crushed when a steel support beam came down under a collapsing roof.) To make matters worse, Early Warning did not have replacements for the patterns and dies. Both Early Warning and Family Owned were shocked to learn that the loss of this property was not covered under the insurance program of either firm.

This loss represents a failure on the part of both organizations to identify an exposure (for Early Warning, personal property located off-premises; for Family Owned, personal property in its care, custody, and control). If Early Warning had recognized the exposure, it could have used the risk control technique of duplication, buying and storing at its premises a second set of patterns and dies. It could have promptly shipped them to Family Owned (or another supplier), enabling Family Owned to continue production of the alarm cases.

From a risk financing standpoint, if Early Warning had chosen to insure this property, it could have easily done so under its existing property insurance policy. Alternatively, it could have transferred the risk of loss of this property to Family Owned under a contract. Assuming that the contract was valid, Early Warning would have a right to recover the cost of replacing the lost property from Family Owned. To make certain that Family Owned would have the resources to honor this contractual assumption of liability, Early Warning could have insisted that Family Owned purchase appropriate insurance coverage.

A larger problem arose when Family Owned was unable to operate for six months after the hurricane damage. The firm had dramatically underestimated the costs to replace its real and personal property and had to arrange to borrow the needed funds. Family Owned had much competition for funds and for the material and contractors with which to rebuild because so many businesses and homes had been damaged. Because Family Owned was the sole supplier of the alarm cases, Early Warning was unable to produce the alarms and to fill the orders it had accepted under its contract with its largest customer. The customer subsequently decided to purchase alarms in the future from Early Warning's largest competitor.

By identifying and analyzing the exposure presented by the use of Family Owned as a sole source of supply, Early Warning could have diversified its source of supply, preventing or at least reducing the net income losses associated with the shutdown of Family Owned. In addition, this potential loss could have been covered under Early Warning's business income insurance policy. Exhibit 6-3 summarizes the techniques for treating Early Warning's exposures.

Exhibit 6-3
Techniques for Treating Early Warning's Exposures

Risk Control
- Duplication
  - manufacture and keep a set of patterns and dies in another location
  - diversify source of supply of alarm cases

Risk Financing
- Insurance
- Noninsurance transfer

EVALUATION

These three brief case studies emphasize the usefulness of the risk management process. From for-profit service and manufacturing firms to the technical departments of nonprofit healthcare facilities, all kinds of organizations can benefit from the systematic application of the risk management process.

Clearly, the most crucial step in the process is the first one, identifying and analyzing loss exposures. Merely classifying the exposures an organization faces into the four types of loss exposures—property loss exposures, net income loss exposures, liability loss exposures, and personnel loss exposures—helps to assure thoroughness in exposure identification and analysis. Virtually *all* loss exposures can be classified in this way.

But all of the steps in the process are, of course, important. The rule of thumb that each identified and analyzed exposure should be treated with at least one risk control and one risk financing technique helps to assure that a sufficient variety of treatment techniques will be considered and provides some guidance for their selection and implementation.

The identification of Failsafe's personnel exposure would have done the firm little good if the exposure had continued to be untreated. The director of the animal lab had certainly identified and treated the lab's property exposure, but he had done so without analyzing the exposure and had thus implemented an inappropriate and insufficient treatment, a risk financing technique on its own. The purchase of property insurance by Early Warning or Family Owned to cover the cost of replacing the patterns and dies would have been of little value if not combined with the risk control technique of duplication, assuring the continuity of production.

These brief case studies also help to underscore the value of risk management for individuals, organizations, communities, and economies. Losses are too often discussed as abstractions, but they are not abstract. They are the actual destruction or impairment of lives, health or wealth. The risk management process, systematically and thoroughly applied, can do much to limit not only the anxiety that necessarily arises from the chance of loss but also the harm done by losses that occur despite the best efforts to prevent them.

REVIEW QUESTIONS AND EXERCISES

1. If Al Smyth, working with an insurance agent or broker, had *identified* Failsafe's personnel exposure, how should they have gone about *analyzing* that exposure?

2. The purchase of life insurance was one method of treating Failsafe's personnel exposure. Briefly describe one risk control technique that could also treat Failsafe's personnel exposure.

3. The Failsafe case indicates that two risk control techniques, separation and duplication, could have been used to treat Failsafe's personnel exposure. Distinguish between separation and duplication. Do you think either one of these techniques would have been sufficient? Give reasons for your answer.

4. Stella Evans recommends that StateMed's security office be informed of potential thefts. Is this a risk control technique, a risk financing technique, or neither? Explain the reasons for your answer.

5. The recommendations for treating the property exposure at StateMed refer to productivity and employee morale in addition to the cost of replacing or repairing lost or damaged property. Would you describe the chance of reduced productivity and low employee morale as a pure risk, a speculative risk, or neither? Give reasons for your answer.

6. Risk management is sometimes said to bring objectivity to potentially emotional situations. Based on Stella Evans' handling of the director of the animal lab's problem, would you say this statement is true or false? Explain your answer.

7. Early Warning's use of Family Owned as the sole supplier of its cases might be described as a hazard rather than a peril or cause of loss. Explain.

8. Two types of loss exposures arose from Early Warning's ownership of and need for the use of the patterns and dies. Name those two types of exposures.

9. The Early Warning case described the use of a noninsurance transfer as one risk financing method of treating Early Warning's property loss exposure. Describe at least one advantage and one disadvantage of the use of this treatment technique by Early Warning.

ANSWERS TO ASSIGNMENT 6 QUESTIONS

1. Al Smyth, working with the insurance agent or broker, should have examined organizational objectives and compared the responsibilities of the key executives to the accomplishment of those objectives. This approach would indicate what the organization would have been unable to do should it incur a specific personnel loss. Al and the insurance broker should also have examined how the potential personnel losses would have affected profit, continuous operations, stability of earnings, and growth—all of which are linked to the organizational objectives.

2. Risk control techniques that could also treat Fairsafe's personnel exposure include the following:

    *   Separation—Requiring key executives to fly on separate aircraft

    *   Duplication—Identifying potential replacements for key executives and encouraging succession planning

3. Separation involves separating the key executives when they are exposed to possible risks, like air travel. Duplication involves having backups, which could mean, for example, having a succession plan in effect. These techniques combined would probably be adequate.

4. Neither. Simply notifying the security office of the thefts is not in itself a risk control technique. However, if the security office implemented procedures to reduce losses (for example, to check packages taken in and out of the lab or to install video cameras), then these procedures would be risk control techniques. It is not a risk financing technique because it involves no financing.

5. Reduced productivity is a loss and, therefore, a pure risk because there is no chance of gain. Low employee morale is often associated with reduced productivity and would result in a loss or, at best, no loss. Therefore, it also is a pure risk.

6. This statement is true. Because of Stella's recommendations, the director's immediate budget problem was solved, and in the long term, he would reduce losses. Having real solutions to problems relieves the emotional strain often associated with them.

7. By using Family Owned as the only provider of patterns and dies in its alarm systems, Early Warning increased the likelihood of net income loss. Early Warning could not continue to manufacture its products without the metal cases supplied solely by Family Owned.

8. Two types of loss exposures that arose from Early Warning's ownership of and need for the use of the patterns and dies are the following:

    *   Net income exposure resulting from Early Warning's inability to produce its products without the patterns and dies

    *   Property loss exposure resulting from Family Owned having the patterns and dies needed to produce the metal cases for Early Warning.

9. By using non-insurance transfer as one risk financing method, Early Warning could have transferred the risk of loss of the patterns and dies to Family Owned under a contract. This action would give Early Warning the right to recover the cost of replacing the patterns and dies (advantage). However, Early Warning would still incur a net income loss because it could not resume product production until the patterns and dies had been replaced (disadvantage).

About Institute Exams

Exam questions are based on the educational objectives stated in the course guide. The exam is designed to measure whether you have met those educational objectives. The exam does not test every educational objective. Instead, it tests over a balanced sample of educational objectives.

TYPES OF EXAM QUESTIONS

The Correct-Answer Type

In this type of question, the question stem is followed by four responses, one of which is absolutely correct. Select the *correct* answer.

> Which one of the following persons evaluates requests for insurance and determines which applicants are accepted and which are rejected?
>
> a. The premium auditor
>
> b. The loss control representative
>
> c. The underwriter
>
> d. The risk manager

The Best-Answer Type

In this type of question, the question stem is followed by four responses, only one of which is best, given the statement made or facts provided in the stem. Select the *best* answer.

Several people within an insurer might be involved in determining whether an applicant for insurance is accepted. Which one of the following is primarily responsible for determining whether an applicant for insurance is accepted?

a. The loss control representative

b. The customer service representative

c. The underwriter

d. The premium auditor

The Incomplete-Statement or Sentence-Completion Type

In this type of question, the last part of the question stem consists of a portion of a statement rather than a direct question. Select the phrase that *correctly* or *best* completes the sentence.

Residual market plans designed for individuals who have been unable to obtain insurance on their personal property in the voluntary market are called

a. VIN plans.

b. Self-insured retention plans.

c. Premium discount plans.

d. FAIR plans.

"All of the Above" Type

In this type of question, only one of the first three answers could be correct, or all three might be correct, in which case the best answer would be "All of the above." Read all the answers and select the *best* answer.

When a large commercial insured's policy is up for renewal, who is likely to provide input to the renewal decision process?

a. The underwriter

b. The loss control representative

c. The producer

d. All of the above

"All of the following, EXCEPT:" Type

In this type of question, responses include three correct answers and one answer that is incorrect or is clearly the least correct. Select the *incorrect* or *least correct* answer.

All of the following adjust insurance claims, EXCEPT:

a. Insurer claim representatives

b. Premium auditors

c. Producers

d. Independent adjusters

INTRODUCTION TO RISK MANAGEMENT
SAMPLE EXAM

1. All of the following are ways in which the risk management process attempts to manage risk, EXCEPT:

   a. Classifying loss exposures into different types

   b. Trying to decrease the frequency or severity of losses

   c. Trying to prevent losses

   d. Paying for those losses that occur

2. A cause of loss is also called a

   a. Risk.

   b. Peril.

   c. Loss exposure.

   d. Hazard.

3. The amount of revenues over expenses that is generated in a specific accounting period is

   a. Gross income.

   b. Net income.

   c. Capital surplus.

   d. Insurance reserves.

4. All of the following are types of loss exposures, EXCEPT:

   a. Liability

   b. Personnel

   c. Investments

   d. Net income

5. Real property includes which of the following?

   a. Buildings

   b. Furniture

   c. Inventory

   d. All of the above

6. Important benefits of risk management include which of the following?

    a.   Peace of mind

    b.   Prevention of losses

    c.   Reduction of the financial consequences of losses

    d.   All of the above

7. For society as a whole, having fewer and less costly losses means that

    a.   Insurers have more money from which to pay claims.

    b.   More funds are available for other uses that can spur economic growth.

    c.   All citizens are protected from the costly consequences imposed by loss.

    d.   Uncertainty about insurance is reduced.

8. How do small business owners, chief financial officers, insurance agents, and business consultants differ from private individuals in making risk management decisions, if at all?

    a.   They are aware of the need to manage risks and use a systematic method of handling risks.

    b.   They are trained in specific loss reduction methods.

    c.   They are in a better position financially to respond to risk and can use business capital for loss control purposes.

    d.   There is no fundamental difference because loss exposures exit for business entities as well as for private individuals.

9. Which one of the following is the best method for a risk manager to use when attempting to identify an organization's real and personal property that is exposed to loss?

    a.   Review the organization's tax returns

    b.   Conduct a personal inspection

    c.   Develop a flowchart

    d.   Research records of losses to other organizations

10. Net income and personnel loss exposures are most relevant for the risk management of

    a.   Individuals.

    b.   Society in general.

    c.   Organizations.

    d.   Materials and resources.

11. All of the following are appropriate risk financing techniques for handling personnel loss exposures in an organization, EXCEPT:

    a. Disability insurance

    b. Life insurance

    c. Auto liability insurance

    d. Health insurance

12. For most individuals, all of the following risk management techniques are appropriate for managing the risks related to the use of an automobile, EXCEPT:

    a. Segregation of exposures

    b. Avoidance

    c. Loss prevention

    d. Risk financing

13. Purchasing insurance is an example of what kind of risk management activity?

    a. Technical

    b. Sales

    c. Managerial

    d. Accounting

14. Which one of the following provides a risk manager with important information for monitoring an organization's risk management program?

    a. Sales report

    b. Annual budget

    c. Audited financial statement

    d. Sales expense accounts

15. Implementing the chosen risk management technique requires two types of activities. Those two activities are technical and

    a. Operational.

    b. Financial.

    c. Managerial.

    d. Organizational.

16. A successful risk management program

    a.   Is not as important for a nonprofit organization as it is for a for-profit organization.

    b.   Does not need to address the needs of internal customers.

    c.   Has as its primary goal to purchase insurance at the lowest possible cost.

    d.   Is attuned to the organization's culture and aligned with its goals.

17. All of the following are costs of risk, EXCEPT:

    a.   Reductions in an organization's actual losses

    b.   Things of value damaged or destroyed in accidents

    c.   Loss of profits that could have been gained in activities avoided as being too risky

    d.   Resources devoted to managing risk, that could have been employed elsewhere

18. Which one of the following skills is needed most to be a successful risk manager?

    a.   Computer

    b.   Insurance rating

    c.   Communication

    d.   Accounting

19. Which one of the following is the best way for an organization to evaluate the performance of a risk management program?

    a.   Compare the organization's loss experience from year to year

    b.   Compare the organization's costs from year to year

    c.   Measure the number of specific activities accomplished within a time period

    d.   Solicit regular feedback from other managers in the organization

20. All of the following are pre-loss objectives in a risk management program, EXCEPT:

    a.   Tolerable uncertainty

    b.   Humanitarian conduct

    c.   Profitability

    d.   Legality

21. A risk manager is concerned about the possibility that a fire at her organization's building will cause an interruption of the organization's business activity. What type of loss exposure does this represent?

    a.   Property

    b.   Liability

    c.   Personnel

    d.   Net income

22. Which one of the following is the risk management technique that is being used when an organization accepts a large deductible on a property insurance policy?

    a.   Segregation of exposures

    b.   Retention

    c.   Risk financing transfer

    d.   Contractual transfer for risk control

23. Which one of the following statements best describes the overall role of a risk manager in a for-profit business entity?

    a.   The risk manager develops a risk control and financing plan that contributes positively to earnings.

    b.   The risk manager develops a risk control and financing plan that eliminates uncertainty for management.

    c.   The risk manager implements the least costly risk control and financing program for the entire organization.

    d.   The risk manager limits its risk control spending to accounting periods of expected increased profitability.

24. Steady Corporation has shown a profit and paid quarterly dividends to its stockholders for the past 20 years. Which one of the following post-loss objectives for risk management best recognizes the importance of continued dividend payments to stockholders?

    a.   Growth

    b.   Profitability

    c.   Legality

    d.   Tolerable uncertainty

25. The city of Chester is sponsoring a 10-mile run in connection with the opening of its newest park and recreation center. All entrants (or guardians) are required to sign an agreement holding the city harmless for any injuries occurring during the race. These requirements are evidence of implementation of which one of the following risk management techniques?

    a.   Contractual transfer for risk financing

    b.   Contractual transfer for risk control

    c.   Avoidance

    d.   Segregation of exposures

26. TNT, Inc., uses a contractor to perform particularly hazardous activities involving blasting operations. In using a hold harmless agreement to transfer the responsibility for losses arising from the blasting operations to the contractor, TNT, Inc., has shifted its financial responsibility through

    a.   A waiver.

    b.   A risk financing transfer.

    c.   An insurance contract.

    d.   A funded transfer mechanism.

27. The risk management process is

    a. Finished when all the loss exposures have been identified.

    b. Finished when all the loss exposures have been identified and analyzed.

    c. Finished when all the loss exposures have been treated.

    d. Never finished.

28. All of the following are steps in the risk management process, EXCEPT:

    a. Identifying and analyzing loss exposures

    b. Implementing a selected technique for treating loss exposures

    c. Outlining objectives for growth of the risk management staff

    d. Monitoring results and considering the need for improvement

29. Which one of the following statements best describes how risk management is most effectively used by large business organizations?

    a. Risk management identifies predictable ways to pay for losses that occur.

    b. Risk management's priority is limiting the consequences of an actual loss.

    c. Risk management identifies activities that present loss exposures and recommends avoidance.

    d. Risk management techniques are best used as a supplement to insurance.

30. Methods of identifying loss exposures include which of the following?

    a. Hedging

    b. Flowcharts

    c. Separation

    d. Transfer

31. Tom is a general contractor who is building an office complex. Tom requires all subcontractors to agree to indemnify and hold him harmless for any liability that he might incur because of injuries to third parties that are caused by the subcontractor. Which one of the following risk control techniques has Tom implemented?

    a. Avoidance

    b. Contractual transfer for risk control

    c. Segregation of loss exposures

    d. Separation of loss exposures

32. Bill's personal auto policy is up for renewal. His agent recommends that Bill should increase the deductible from $100 to $500. If Bill has an accident, he can afford to pay the deductible from current income. Which one of the following statements describes the risk financing technique that Bill is implementing regarding the deductible?

   a. Bill is implementing retention with current expensing of losses for the deductible amount.

   b. Bill is implementing retention and is creating an unfunded reserve for the deductible amount.

   c. Bill is implementing retention and is creating a funded reserve for the deductible amount.

   d. Bill is implementing retention and practicing hedging for the deductible amount.

33. Fun Fashions, a clothing manufacturer, stores inventory in several warehouses at different locations. This is an example of which one of the following techniques for treating loss exposures?

   a. Separation

   b. Duplication

   c. Avoidance

   d. Transfer

34. Which one of the following is most likely to implement avoidance?

   a. A young couple who are considering buying their first house

   b. An entrepreneur who is seeking investors for her Internet sales site

   c. A regional advertising firm that is offered a lucrative contract with strict delivery deadlines

   d. A large corporation that is considering adding a new product to its existing 100-item product line

35. Which one of the following is a primary reason why a risk manager monitors the risk management program?

   a. To continuously improve the program

   b. To weigh the effectiveness and economy of all available techniques in light of stated objectives

   c. To coordinate recommendations for risk control and risk financing that appear separate and distinct

   d. To measure the financial consequences of a loss for a specific person or organization

36. Which of the following is (are) true about measuring results of a risk management program?

   a. Results of loss experience from year to year are most accurately measured using relatively short time periods.

   b. When doing a cost benefit analysis of risk management, the costs are difficult to measure while the benefits are easy to measure.

   c. The results of a risk management program can be measured by using a combination of methods, including a comparison of loss experience from year to year and a cost benefit analysis.

   d. All of the above

37. Which of the following explain(s) the relationship between the risk manager and the organization?

    a. The risk manager has a vision or emphasis that supports the organization's corporate vision.

    b. The risk manager focuses on streamlining the operations of an organization's external customers.

    c. The activities of the risk manager are generally performed independently of other managers within the organization.

    d. All of the above

38. A waste landfill operation is subject to unannounced, periodic inspections by various governmental agencies. Which one of the following categories of pre-loss objectives should support the entity's goal to be in compliance with the rules of these agencies?

    a. Economy of operations

    b. Tolerable uncertainty

    c. Survival

    d. Legality

39. One of the objectives of Berk's School District is to meet the needs of the community while minimizing risks for the district. The parents at one school want to raise money to pay for playground equipment. Which one of the following statements describes the first step the risk manager should take before the district votes on whether to install the equipment?

    a. The risk manager should urge the district to ban the equipment, because it presents a new loss exposure.

    b. The risk manager should investigate the common types of accidents that occur on playground equipment.

    c. The risk manager should recommend that a list of safety rules be posted by the equipment.

    d. The risk manager should investigate the cost of additional necessary insurance.

40. Which one of the following is a risk financing technique that includes a transfer of risk?

    a. Commercial insurance

    b. An unfunded reserve

    c. Borrowing funds to pay for losses

    d. Current expensing of losses

ANSWERS TO INTRODUCTION TO RISK MANAGEMENT SAMPLE EXAM

1.	A	21.	D
2.	B	22.	B
3.	B	23.	A
4.	C	24.	B
5.	A	25.	B
6.	D	26.	B
7.	B	27.	D
8.	A	28.	C
9.	B	29.	B
10.	C	30.	B
11.	C	31.	B
12.	B	32.	A
13.	A	33.	A
14.	B	34.	D
15.	C	35.	A
16.	D	36.	C
17.	A	37.	A
18.	C	38.	D
19.	D	39.	B
20.	C	40.	A

Glossary

KEY WORDS AND PHRASES DEFINED OR EXPLAINED

The numbers in parentheses refer to the assignments in which the key word or phrase appears.

Avoidance

Choosing not to own an asset or engage in an activity that gives rise to the possibility of loss. (2)

Benefits of risk management

- Prevention of losses
- Reduction of the financial consequences of losses and reduction of lost opportunities
- Peace of mind (1) (4)

Captive insurance company

An insurance company established as a subsidiary of an organization to provide that organization with insurance. A captive insurance company is a risk financing technique. (4)

Contractual transfer for risk control

Transferring the legal and financial responsibility for a loss from one individual or organization to another. (2)

Costs of risk

1. The lives, property, income, or other things of value damaged or destroyed in accidents.

2. The loss of potential profits or benefits that could have been gained through the ownership of assets or participation in activities that were avoided as "too risky."

3. The cost of risk management. (4)

Costs of risk management
The resources devoted to managing accidental losses. (4)

Customers
The recipients of products, information, or services. (3)

Hazard
Anything that increases the possible frequency or severity of a loss. (2)

Insurance
A system by which a risk is transferred by a person or an organization to an insurance company in exchange for a periodic payment, the insurance premium. (2)

Liability
Liability means that an individual or organization is legally responsible for the injury or damage suffered by another person or organization. (1)

Line authority
Authority that grants the person or department the power to do specific things or to authorize others to do them. (3)

Loss
A loss occurs when an item of property or a right owned by a person or an organization has declined in value, or a capacity to perform has been diminished. (1)

Loss exposure
The possibility of accidental loss with measurable financial consequences. (1)

Loss frequency
Refers to how often losses occur and is used to predict the likelihood of similar losses in the future. (1)

Loss prevention
Reducing the frequency of a particular loss. (2)

Loss reduction
Decreasing the severity of a particular loss. (2)

Loss severity
Refers to the amount of damage resulting from losses and is used to predict how costly future losses are likely to be. (1)

Managerial risk management activities
Activities that require the cooperation of other managers besides the risk manager. (3)

Net income
The amount of revenues over expenses that is generated in a specific accounting period. (1)

Peril

A cause of loss. (1)

Personal property

Everything but real property. Examples: furniture, fixtures, and inventory. (1)

Personnel loss exposure

Employing personnel represents a personnel loss exposure through the possible death, disability, or injury of an employee. (1)

Post-loss objectives

The minimal condition an organization's senior management can accept following the most severe foreseeable loss.

Examples:

1. Survival

2. Continuity of operations

3. Profitability

4. Stability of earnings

5. Growth

6. Humanitarian conduct (4)

Pre-loss objectives

Objectives that have value whether or not a loss occurs.

Examples:

1. Economy of operations

2. Tolerable uncertainty

3. Legality

4. Humanitarian conduct (4)

Property loss exposure

The possibility of accidental loss to real or personal property. (1)

Pure risk

Can only result in a loss or no loss; presents no opportunity for gain. (1)

Real property

Land, buildings, and other structures attached to the land. (1)

Retention

Individuals or organizations plan to generate the funds to pay for losses themselves. (2)

Risk

Uncertainty about whether a loss will occur. (1)

Risk management

The process to best handle uncertainty about whether losses will occur. (1)

Risk management benefits

- Prevention of losses

- Reduction of the financial consequences of losses

- Peace of mind (1) (4)

Segregation of exposures

Can be accomplished by:

1. **Separation**

   Relies on the dispersal of a particular activity or asset over more than one location.

Example:

When the owners of a clothing manufacturer store their inventory in a number of different warehouses at different locations, a fire at any one warehouse would not destroy the firm's entire inventory.

2. Duplication

Relies on having backups, spares, or duplicates of crucial assets readily available.

Example:

Keeping a spare tire in the trunk of your car. (2)

Speculative risk

Can result in loss, no loss, or gain. (1)

Staff authority

Authority that limits the person's or department's power to giving advice to others. (3)

Suppliers

People or organizations who provide products, information, or services to others. (3)

Technical risk management activities

Activities that are related directly to the risk management function and can be carried out by the person or department that performs that function in an organization. (3)

Transfer

Shifts the financial responsibility for losses from one party to another through a contract. (2)

Index